Praise For

YOUR B.R.A.N.D. UNLEASHED

"*Your B.R.A.N.D. Unleashed* is a great roadmap for leaders who want to create a top-notch customer experience and drive their business ahead of the competition. Lisa just gets it!"

—**Barbara Corcoran**, Founder of The Corcoran Group and Shark on ABC's Shark Tank

"This book is a treasure for anyone who wants to build their brand, enhance their organization, and increase their successful results."

—**Dr. Nido Qubein**, Author of *How To Communicate Like A Pro and Stairway to Success: The Complete Blueprint for Personal and Professional Achievement*, President of High Point University

"If you truly want to master marketing and attract more high-value, high-paying clients, then you absolutely need to read Lisa's book and take her advice on branding. As someone who has made all things marketing, influence, and sales my life's work, I can say without a doubt that everything Lisa has put in her book is spot on and should be followed to the letter. I also know Lisa personally and vouch for her as an advisor. She is a high-caliber consultant with impeccable integrity. If you get a chance to work with her, take it."

—**Robin Robins**, CEO of Technology Marketing Toolkit

"After nearly 30 years of building organizations that deliver the Ultimate Client Experience (UCE), I've learned that client loyalty is forged through the emotional connections we create in every interaction—often in the simplest moments that might seem insignificant at the time. In ***Your B.R.A.N.D. Unleashed***, Lisa Shorr masterfully captures this idea, guiding you through nine proven strategies that transform the client experience into a powerful tool for long-term success. What resonated with me is how Shorr emphasizes that your brand is the culmination of every employee's brand. Her book is a roadmap for creating the alignment needed to ensure everyone in your organization contributes to a cohesive and powerful brand presence. With actionable insights on communicating with empathy, delivering consistent value, and fostering deep client connections, this book is a must-read for anyone serious about elevating their personal and professional brand. Shorr shows how to retain customers and turn them into loyal advocates for your business by intentionally enhancing every touchpoint with clients."

—**Tim Hebert**, Author of *The Intentional Leader*, Founder Dirigo

"Having experienced the rapid and enduring positive transformation that Lisa's corporate brand coaching and phone skills did for my team and my business, I was looking forward to reading her book, *Your BRAND Unleashed*. The book did not disappoint! Lisa manages to replicate the magic of her in-person coaching by providing a straightforward roadmap to building enduring trust and credibility with your customers. This easy to read and entertaining book is full of practical advice, actionable strategies, and real-world examples that will motivate and help you take charge of your personal brand and lead your team with confidence. Whether you're a seasoned business owner running a large corporation, or just hired your first employee, this book is a must-read for building team buy-in what your brand stands for and taking your business to the next level!"

—**Dr. Sarah Levy**, Founder and Owner of Facial Aesthetics Center

"Your B.R.A.N.D. Unleashed by Lisa Shorr is the ultimate guide for building your personal brand. Lisa is a master of her craft, and this book is a transformational blueprint filled with practical and actionable steps you can take to build your personal brand and ultimately grow your business. From setting S.M.A.R.T. goals, having the right mindset, mastering communication skills to dressing to impress, Lisa guides you to success."

—**Derek Anderson**, Entrepreneur, CEO, BizTek Solutions, Inc.

YOUR B.R.A.N.D. UNLEASHED

YOUR B.R.A.N.D. UNLEASHED

9 PROVEN STRATEGIES THAT BUILD TRUST AND MAINTAIN LASTING CLIENT LOYALTY

LISA A. SHORR

Your B.R.A.N.D. Unleashed
9 Proven Strategies That Build Trust and Maintain Lasting Client Loyalty

For information about this title contact the publisher:

Lisa Shorr/Shorr Success
https://shorrsuccess.com/your-brand-unleashed

ISBNs:
979-8-9899497-0-0 (softcover)
979-8-9899497-1-7 (eBook)

Printed in the United States of America

Cover and Interior design: 1106 Design

To Grandma Belle, my original Image Coach. You made thousands of women feel valued, beautiful, and inspired, including me, through your relentless pursuit of building your client base, by selling one skin cleanser, one moisturizer, one lipstick at a time.

Every visit you'd ask in an interested tone: "Lis, how are you . . . ?" I always replied with a wide smile, "I'm just fine."

If you were with me today, I'd say, "I'm feeling proud Grandma, here's a copy of my new book for you; it's all about building empathetic relationships, just like ours." Love you, Grandma.

TABLE OF CONTENTS

Author's Note

The stories in this book come from my decades in the business community either as an employee or a business owner. For confidentiality, I've changed names and some details. I've also gathered insights and statistics from various sources and experts. I identify and provide links to their websites.

INTRODUCTION

Repeat after me: "Technical expertise alone won't build my business."

This is our mantra while reading this book.

Did you start your business because you are passionate about the product or service you offer? Did your business begin as an idea or hobby that slowly started to bring on one client, then two, then three, and before you knew it, you needed to hire an employee to help with the burgeoning amount of work on your plate?

Your excitement rises when you bring on a second, then a third employee as your client base grows. Perhaps you began to invest in the latest equipment and software needed to be more productive to run your growing business more efficiently. I can feel your excitement. The revenue generated by growth is exhilarating!

Envision this: You analyze your business growth and realize it mostly comes from client referrals. As you sip a cup of coffee, a feeling of satisfaction sweeps over you as you think how loyal your clients are. With pride, you attribute this growth to your emphasis on making sure your team members are masters in their trade. Of course they are, you invest heavily in educational trade shows, virtual training programs, and industry certifications for them.

But then, imagine for a minute that enthusiasm for your growing business is tested after you receive a phone call from a distressed client threatening to leave you. With sweat forming on your brow and your brain sifting through your mental database of recent interactions with this client, you ask, "Please tell me what's going on?" Expecting to hear your client complain about a lack of competence in your team's technical ability, you're dumbfounded to hear: "I just don't feel like your company understands my needs or makes me feel important." Needs? Importance? How do you respond to this?

You take a deep breath and ask your client to please provide an example or two. In a disappointed tone, your client responds with: "Every time I call, your team members act like they have no idea who I am." Or "I don't like the way Joe speaks to me. He always sounds so frustrated."

You thank your client for their candor and for raising these concerns. After a lengthy discussion that resolves the issue, you hang up. With your head and heart pounding, you sigh. *Whew, crisis averted. I've got to get back to work.*

Imagine a few weeks later, another frustrated client call is transferred to you. This time, the outcome leaves you feeling befuddled and angry. Your client says they're going with another provider. Feeling pangs of shock and exasperation for being blindsided, you blurt, "What are you talking about? We give you great service."

"I never hear from you. Besides, I wanted to test out a new software and you said, 'I hope we can figure it out.' I had no confidence that you could handle the project, so I went with someone who could."

Sitting behind your desk, bleary-eyed from this call and remembering the call from a few weeks before, you think about $10,000 a year in lost revenue. How in the world are you going to make that up? You can't afford to lose any more business.

Let's look at these client calls. The client feels you don't understand their needs: They never hear from you, and you've unintentionally communicated a lack of competence to meet their project needs. This has nothing to do with your technical ability and everything to do with communication skills.

Is your tech zone your comfort zone? Would you rather put off dealing with that disgruntled client or rogue employee? Maybe you feel like you have no problems at all—it's everyone else who needs an attitude adjustment! Don't get me wrong; I know how important it is to constantly evolve your craft and stay ahead of the curve. Training and certifications are critical investments in your business. However, when a client decides to leave you or a prospect selects your competitor over you, ask yourself: "Why did they really make that decision?" You may explain it this way: "Oh, they're cheap and don't want to pay," or maybe "They're so unreasonable. They don't appreciate all I do for them."

Here's the hard truth: You didn't make your client ***feel*** that their needs are important. The critical word here is "feel." Relationships are built on feelings. Ideally, the employee, client, or prospect feels trust, confidence, and that all important sense that "I made the right choice," by selecting you as their employer or business partner. Once doubt enters the picture and trust is broken, it's extremely hard, if not impossible, to win back their confidence.

Why Read This Book?

My mission with *Your B.R.A.N.D. Unleashed* is to accelerate your business to the next level. How? By shifting your mindset from believing technical skills are all you and your team need to focus on to grow your business. You also need to understand that interpersonal and communication skills are the powerful drivers that set the true foundation for fruitful, profitable, long-lasting relationships. As your coach, I will give you the step-by-step process to turn your tech-focused team into intentional **Brand-Building Rockstars** that your clients rave about, so prospects seek you out.

In ***Your B.R.A.N.D. Unleashed*** you will find activities, client examples, team discussion questions, and interactive videos geared to reinforce your new skills and set you up for unlimited success.

It's time to jump out of your comfort zone and join me on the next step of your journey to polish your **communication skills** and build **a memorable Personal Brand** that exudes confidence, empathy, and integrity. Envision your existing clients buying more from you and sending you referrals. Imagine prospects calling you because of your stellar brand!

So roll up your sleeves and let's take the first step together . . .

What Is a Personal Brand and Why Should You Care?

What Is a Personal Brand?

When you think of retired football great Tom Brady, what's the first thought that comes to mind? Is it seven Super Bowl rings . . . one of the greatest quarterbacks of all time (the G.O.A.T.) . . . an inspirational leader? The list could go on and on.

If I mentioned Elon Musk—what would your reaction be? Genius . . . space pioneer . . . revolutionizing the electric car industry? Are we close to sharing the same thoughts?

Over and over, when I ask my clients, what do you think a Personal Brand is, they typically offer similar responses: how you present yourself . . . your look and personality . . . a great first impression.

This is only half of the definition. The second key component to a strong Personal Brand is often overlooked: what others say about you when you are not physically in the room. It's what makes you both memorable and magnetic. Most of us don't know Tom Brady personally. However, if you and I were surveyed together, I bet we would share many of the same sentiments.

A powerful Personal Brand has two key components:

1. A strong executive presence

2. Consistent empathetic behavior

Your executive presence is your ability to walk into a room and immediately command attention, not demand it. The silent, subliminal message you send says, "Hey, I'm worth listening to!" It could be your professional appearance, your confident voice, your winning smile coupled with eye contact, or your ability to stay cool under pressure. Whatever feelings you evoke, your audience admires you and is "all ears" when you speak. They believe you will teach them, inspire them, and validate them.

While executive presence is more of an in-person experience, a memorable Personal Brand is formed when you pay attention to how you emotionally connect to your audience using empathetic behavior. Tom Brady didn't just lead while on the football field. He has taken great care to curate a winning team mindset and culture in his various businesses, publicly takes care of himself through strict nutrition, and is perceived to be a devoted father. His fans around the world proudly don T-shirts and jackets with Brady's bold #12 on their backs, feeling his positive energy and a sense of pride for all that Brady represents.

Why Should You Care?

There is a key word I've mentioned multiple times so far. Can you guess it? It's "feeling." If you guessed right, I'm giving you a virtual high-five! If you didn't, no worries. I'm going to mention this pivotal word several more times throughout this book.

So why should you care about your Personal Brand? **Because perception is reality**. I like to say, "Other people's perception is their reality." Perception is built based on our *value judgments*. Value judgments are our views and perspectives, formed from a variety of factors that include our upbringing, culture, social circles, and educational experiences, to name a few. When building a strong Personal Brand, it's essential to understand that you and I were each raised differently. Our experiences and perceptions will often be different. So, when building your brand, you must ask yourself, **"How do I want to be perceived by others?"**

How your audience perceives you often determines the future of your relationship. Will your prospect sign their new quote? Will you be invited to speak? Will your client renew their contract? Will your prospect go with a competitor? Internally, will your employee leave your business for greener pastures? These decisions incorporate your technical ability, yet your outcome is primarily due to a feeling of trust and a belief in your ability to understand *your clients' needs* and help them build *their* business. That trust will either grow or be broken due to a lack of consistency in your Personal Brand.

At the end of the day, building your brand and trying to positively influence others to select your product or service takes *intentionality*. I'm not saying I want you to lose your authenticity. Rather, how do you take your unique qualities and use them to your advantage to set you and your business apart from your competition?

Lisa's Two I's for Image—Intention vs. Interpretation

Several years ago, a super tech-savvy engineer worked for my IT company. When we interviewed Donald, we were dazzled by his tech knowledge; it was beyond that of many of my other engineers. What a find, we thought! A few clients had especially complicated networks, and Donald's tech skills could easily tackle the challenges. But while his technical skills were top-notch, there was an issue with Donald's communication skills. "Humble" was not in Donald's vocabulary. He had a propensity to speak in an arrogant and exasperated tone, making everyone around him, including me, feel uncomfortable and, frankly, hesitant to ask him any questions or seek updates. We naively thought this issue wouldn't be a problem. Our clients would surely be impressed by his technical ability. And hey, he was on-site to improve networks, not become best friends with our clients.

Within a few weeks of Donald working at client sites, one client had enough. She called our office and said, "Do not send Donald back. I want Gregory instead."

"Why? Are you sure?" I asked, disappointment in my voice.

"Donald makes me feel uncomfortable. He talks to me as if I'm stupid," our client reported.

"But Gregory's not as technically proficient as Donald." I tried to sound as controlled as possible while also trying to quell the panic in my voice.

"I know, but I can talk to Gregory. He's friendly and nice to talk to when he's on-site. Either Donald goes or we go."

This is a classic example of Intention vs. Interpretation. My **intention** was to send my client the BEST, most technically proficient engineer I had on staff. What I hadn't factored in was my client's experience working with Donald and their **interpretation** of his abrasive tone. They completely overlooked his technical talent; it didn't matter. Instead, they threatened to leave us because of how Donald made my client "feel." This was a pivotal realization for me.

Think about experiences you've had where you thought, "That's not what I meant." Or "How in the world did she perceive that?" I have no regrets about Donald. I had to learn a valuable lesson: That sometimes what I think are my good intentions may not be perceived the same way by others.

Another key outcome was that I changed my hiring process. Not only do I now test a candidate's technical aptitude, I've also built in several components to screen for their communication and interpersonal skills. When we're on the fence about a candidate, we now ask, "Will this person be a great cultural fit for our clients and our organization?" If the answer is no, even if the technical ability is there, we move on to the next candidate.

This concept is the foundation of building a strong Personal Brand. Depending on how you want to be perceived by others, your appearance, behavior, and communication skills need to have integrity and be believable. Otherwise, the interpretation could likely be something completely opposite of what you intend.

The Difference—Personal Brands Build Corporate Brands

You know the old question, "What came first, the chicken or the egg?" The answer is often an ambiguous "I'm not sure." What is clear is that you cannot have a trusted Corporate Brand without having strong Personal Brands behind it.

A Corporate Brand is how a business presents itself to its prospects and clients. At the foundation, it represents a business's purpose, core values, mission, and personality. A Corporate Brand becomes desirable when there is trust in the product or service: It has instant brand-name recognition, easy logo identification, and a stellar consumer experience.

The Disney brand is known globally as the "*The Happiest Place on Earth.*" Magic Kingdom is the Most Magical. It's all about the "Disney" experience. I had the honor of attending an animated and interactive keynote led by leadership expert, author, and former head of customer service training at Disney, Doug Lipp. His talk was based on his book, *Disney U—How Disney University Develops the World's Most Engaged, Loyal, and Customer-Centric Employees.* His keynote was a compilation of many of the success strategies Disney teaches its employees in an effort to ensure each patron of any Disney destination has a consistent and magical experience. One key concept Lipp taught our group was "Snow White Never Has a Bad Day." Disney knows that *its employees* have a direct impact on the success of its Corporate Brand. A cranky princess is never OK at Disney!

Your goal as a business owner is to make your target consumers believe in your mission and values and to trust the products and services you offer. Imagine your employees were Disney employees. What experience would you want your clients to have? How would you want them to perceive you and talk about you to their colleagues?

That is why focusing on Personal Branding is so critical. And that is why this book is so crucial. To have a strong Corporate Brand, you must have your employees in alignment with your corporate mission and understand that each action they take either builds a relationship with your consumer or damages it.

CHAPTER 2

A Trusted Brand Starts With S.M.A.R.T. Goals

September 12, 1962, was a day that would change our nation forever. Surrounded by a sea of 35,000 men and women who were constantly wiping their brows as they appeared to be melting in the heat of the day, President John F. Kennedy coolly delivered his iconic speech, "We Choose to Go to the Moon" at Houston's Rice University.

JFK was on a mission to enter the space race with Russia. His first step had been on May 25, 1961, when he spoke to a special joint session of Congress. Gaining approval, his next step was a bigger job to accomplish—to inspire the nation to *agree to* and *pay for* the pursuit of safely sending a man to the moon by the end of the decade. Each word he uttered carried urgency and hope.

In a matter of 46 minutes, to roaring applause and cheers, President Kennedy had set the ultimate in S.M.A.R.T. Goals. Send a man safely to the moon and back by December 31, 1969.

Seven years later, Neil Armstrong stepped foot on the moon—mission accomplished!

Why Set Goals?

Motivational speaker Tony Robbins once said, "Setting goals is the first step in turning the invisible into the visible." I love this statement. Goals turn wishes and dreams into tangible realities. They enable you and me to grow our businesses by proactively incorporating methodical strategies that focus on outcomes versus reactive, aimless activities.

Before I understood the power of setting goals, I always felt like a hamster on a wheel, just running in circles with slow company growth. Once I learned the process I am about to teach you, both of my businesses—Shorr Success and Secure Future Tech Solutions—have grown exponentially in revenue and profitability.

There are so many benefits to setting goals. Here are my top five:

1. **Focus—**S.M.A.R.T. Goals establish clear direction on how you want to grow your business. They help you create a focused plan, evaluate it, and course correct if need be. The alternative? Never seeing that pot of gold at the end of the rainbow.

2. **Team Performance**—Morale builds when every team member feels they are a part of a collective mission and that they have clarity on the direction of the company. This morale boost often leads to a boost in productivity and performance.

3. **Purpose**—With goals to achieve, we develop a sense of purpose and determination to achieve success.

4. **Enhanced Time Management**—S.M.A.R.T. Goals bring focus to those specific tasks and activities that will help you attain your goals versus aimlessly completing tasks with little or no positive results.

5. **Confidence and Satisfaction**—Once you hit one goal, you'll gain confidence and be energized to set another and another.

To build a strong Personal Brand requires intentional strategy. Setting goals puts you on a focused path to achieve success.

Stop Mixing Up Activities for S.M.A.R.T. Goals

The first step in my coaching process is to identify goals for the organization. So often when I ask, "Tell me your goals for this year," I receive one of two answers. It's either "I don't have any" or something vague like "I want to grow my business."

If we focus on the latter statement, I commend you for having the right mindset. Now, I want to get you to a point where you have specific goals in place, so that we can track your progress along the way. Let's identify two S.M.A.R.T Goals.

The acronym S.M.A.R.T. Goals was first introduced in 1981 by George T. Doran in a paper he wrote called "There's a S.M.A.R.T. way to write management's goals and objectives." This methodology for setting goals has been utilized extensively. Over the years, this acronym has taken on a few different forms.

For purposes of this book, we'll use this as our acronym:

S **Specific**—What do you want to achieve?

M **Measurable**—Having a specific metric or precise way to track your success.

A **Attainable**—Can you envision your path to success? Do you see a finish line?

R **Relevant and Realistic**—Will you be able to come close to or, even better, achieve the results you want?

T **Time-Bound**—Giving your goal a deadline will help create urgency and better time management.

Stop! Before you write your goal, make sure it is not an "Activity." An activity is a task that supports your goal.

Let's explore. If you were to tell me, "I want to meet with three clients this month," my response would be, "Great, but why only three? Why not more? What result do you want to achieve after meeting with your clients?"

You might respond, "I want to grow my business."

"OK, now we're making progress," I reply. My next question, and this is where the S.M.A.R.T. Goal would come in, is: "How much do you want to increase your business growth? I want you to provide either a revenue amount or percentage. Also, by when do you want to achieve your growth? End of the quarter? End of the year?"

Once you determine a realistic, quantifiable number or percentage to track and give yourself a deadline within which

CHAPTER 3

Mastering Your Success Mindset

"A frog in the well does not know the great sea."
—Japanese Proverb

Max, the owner of a small IT company, was struggling. The pandemic hit his business hard: It lost nearly $600,000 in top-line revenue in two years. Even worse, he could not seem to grow his overall profits. In fact, they were decreasing over time. His head spun, thinking about the consequences if his business kept shrinking.

After Max attended two webinars with me, I offered him and other attendees a free report called **"Top 12 Reasons Why Your Company Image Is Costing You Money."** (Use this URL to download the report: https://msp.shorrsuccess.com/12reasons)

Writing my free report was part cathartic experience and part a strong effort to help struggling small businesses consider what they can do differently. As therapeutic as it was for me, it also created a defining moment for Max. After reading each of the 12 questions, including "Does your service coordinator sound disinterested when answering the phone?" "Are your clients frustrated because they don't feel important?" "Does the body language of your team create awkward situations?" Max kept nodding his head and saying, "Yes," "Yes," and "Yes" after each question. Max then read about how I designed and implemented my proven B.R.A.N.D. Method with profitable success in my business. Anxious excitement surged through his veins. Max brought his hope, urgency, and my free report to his management team. Each manager agreed that it was time to make a change. Max called me that day to set up a meeting.

Our first virtual meeting commenced. After a discussion about the history of their business, I asked Rachel, Max's controller, to read and interpret this Japanese proverb: "A frog in the well does not know the great sea." I asked Rachel what that meant to her. With a bit of hesitation, Rachel shared her perspective. "I guess it means that we don't know the bigger picture of other departments versus knowing what is going on in our department."

After going around the virtual screen and hearing each member's interpretation—plus a quick google by Max—we came to a consensus: Everyone must know their limitations in work and life. Jumping out of our own well will enable us to gain much needed perspective and education on what is going on in other departments as well as expand our knowledge to make us better leaders.

I closed this candid conversation by adding, "Our time together is all about building strong Personal Brands to be better leaders, improve company culture, and ultimately grow your business. We all need to jump out of that well and swim together, communicate together, and share an understanding of each other—because we are all critical to the success of our business."

This mindset shift from putting each member in a department silo to valuing the importance of each role, set the foundation for Max and his team to evolve from department thinking to understanding the interdependence of each person and the value they bring to the growth of the business. They shifted from thinking "me" to "we" and "us."

Their lightbulb moment shined even brighter when they also understood that it was their people who create strong brands, not just the products and services they offered.

Identify Your Value Words

Let's do an exercise. Take out a pen. Answer this question: "How do you want to be perceived by others?" Please write three to five words that explain how you want your employees, clients, colleagues, and friends to perceive you professionally and personally.

While I want you to list your own, here are a few ideas from my clients to get your gears turning: *compassionate, knowledgeable, friendly, empathetic, dependable.*

List your words in the lines below.

1. ____________ 1 ----------------------------------10

2. ____________ 1 ----------------------------------10

3. ____________ 1 ----------------------------------10

4. ____________ 1 ----------------------------------10

5. ____________ 1 ----------------------------------10

When you have your words, ask yourself, "How consistent am I in living by each word?" Next to your value words, rate yourself on a scale of 1–10. One being, "I am not at all consistent" and 10 being, "I live by this word every day!"

I'm proud of you! This is not an easy task. To build a strong Personal Brand, you first need to identify what is important to you. How do you want to be perceived by others? What do you want to be known for?

Now that you've identified what is important to you, use these words to help guide you in building a Personal Brand that aligns with your value words. I strongly recommend writing these three to five words on a Post-It note and placing them on your desk or your monitor so you can view them every day. These words are meant to inspire you and keep you on track when evolving as a leader. As with setting goals, when building your Personal Brand, track your progress along the way:

- Is my verbal and nonverbal communication in line with my value words?
- Does my appearance align with my value words?
- Is my digital presence building or hurting my brand?

Without this self-awareness, you won't know how to build a Personal Brand that enables you to live your value words each day.

SUCCESS EXERCISE

Do this same exercise with your team. What is important to them? Use their words in ongoing discussions to help build their communication skills and enhance team culture.

3 C's of Image: Consistency + Congruency = Credibility

What makes some Personal Brands memorable and others forgettable? The answer to this is simple (see above); becoming memorable, however, is not. Once you identify your corporate goals and determine your inner core values, now determine if each team member's Personal Brand is consistent and congruent. If each team member achieves these two traits—consistency and congruency—then their Personal Brand has credibility, is deemed trustworthy, and is worth paying attention to. Let's explore each word:

Consistency:

Credibility is built and earned. It starts with your clients and prospects understanding what you do and who you serve.

I have spent the past ten years building my brand credibility as an image and branding expert. My target audience is the small business owner and C-Level executive or manager. Now that I've identified my audience, I must ensure that the coaching I deliver, the words I speak, my appearance, the knowledge I share, my digital presence, as well as my marketing materials, invoices, website, and the contents of this book, are all consistent with my core values and brand.

Our clients love consistency. Think about it—they're loyal to brands they know and are comfortable with. Ask yourself: Why have your longest clients stayed with you? Was it because of your great price? Probably not. I'm confident you'll say you *always* provide them with great service. We are *always* there when they need us. My team *always* makes them feel like VIPs.

CONGRUENCY:

Congruency means that your behavior is in harmony with your communication. You and your team tell one story. When I share my expertise, I tell colleagues that I am a coach and consultant who knows how to build strong Personal Brands. I do not tell my clients that I'm also a graphic artist and website content creator—which I can do. Those abilities do help build brands, but I focus on the "human side" of brand building. I don't want to confuse my prospects with every aspect of what I do. Rule of thumb: **A confused buyer never buys**.

Being perceived as consistent and congruent by a prospect leads to credibility. At the end of the day, a brand's credibility is the deciding factor in the buying process.

Turn Your "Head Trash" Into Growth-Minded Statements

It's time to talk about self-limiting beliefs, specifically yours. Self-limiting beliefs are like a long road full of red lights. Every time you are presented with an opportunity to move forward, your mind won't let you take your foot off the brake. You long for that red light to change to green and to press that gas pedal. However, the best you can muster is a cautious yellow. How can you run your business if your mindset is at a standstill?

How often do you tell yourself that "Clients are cheap and won't accept a price increase" or "My town is too small to grow any larger" or "I'm not good enough to take on this new project?" The self-deprecation could go on and on, but I want you to keep reading, not give up from despair!

The main goal of this book is not to depress you but to get you to shift from self-limiting beliefs to having a growth mindset. So don't give up hope—*keep reading.*

Too often, we let fear hold us back. Fear is an emotion stemming from a belief that an action will be a threat or cause some sort of harm. Many choose to remain a "frog in our own well" and let fear get the better of us.

Growth and resilience come when we choose to face our fears and not run away from them.

Let's see how we commit to moving forward together. Below is a list of limiting beliefs that have come out of my clients' mouths. OK, two came from my own "head trash." Busted!

Let's see how we can transform these beliefs into growth-minded declarations. I'll do the first two and you can try your hand at the rest.

Head Trash	Growth-Minded Statement
People are always cheap.	I haven't done enough to demonstrate my value to the prospect/client.
I can't delegate. I must do it myself.	I am excited for you to learn this new skill. Let me show it to you and then you can take it over yourself.
We've always done it this way.	______ ______ ______
Too many competitors in my area for me to make money.	______ ______ ______
I am afraid to look at my financials.	______ ______ ______
I am afraid my employees will quit if I give them feedback.	______ ______ ______
(Add your self-limiting belief here)	______ ______ ______
(Add your self-limiting belief here)	______ ______ ______

A couple of boxes have been left for you to fill in your own self-limiting beliefs. Listen to yourself talk to others or pay attention to what you are saying in your own mind. Write those statements down, then think: How can I shift this thought to become growth-minded? I encourage you to continue to build this list over time.

Great work! I know this wasn't easy. I am asking you to shift a perception you've probably entertained for most of your life. Moving forward, refer to this exercise. Every time you have a negative thought or perceived roadblock, stop yourself and ask, how can I change my perspective?

SUCCESS EXERCISE

Share this exercise with your entire team. See what other fears and self-limiting beliefs they come up with and how they transform them into new growth-minded declarations. I look forward to hearing what new ideas come from it. Send me a message on LinkedIn (https://www.linkedin.com/in/lisashorr/).

You Are Ready for the B.R.A.N.D. Method—A Step-by-Step Process to Becoming a Brand-Building Rockstar

All right! With your value words identified and your mindset in the right place, let's focus on the process of turning you into a sought-after and influential leader.

After testing the B.R.A.N.D. Method on hundreds of small businesses, including my IT business, I'm excited to now share my system with you.

Here is what I know: The single most important asset of a business, especially a service-based business, are your employees. The experience the client or consumer has with your employees is what makes or breaks your brand.

What makes great employees? The leader they follow. Pause for a moment and think: If employee behavior is modeled after leadership, what type of leader are you?

Humans are driven by emotions. Positive or negative experiences determine the state of corporate culture and brand loyalty.

Too often, leaders are stumped by the perceptions of their employees and clients. Have you ever thought, "Why did they think I was angry? I didn't say I was angry!" or "Why is my client leaving? I thought we gave them great service?" or "We had such great rapport, why did they go with our competitor?"

You can infer many reasons from their perceptions. You can even play the "blame game," thinking you said or did nothing wrong. Perception is their reality and what they believe. It's critical to be very intentional and strategic when building relationships.

My B.R.A.N.D Method teaches you how to build and unleash your Personal Brand by concentrating on your appearance, behavior, and communication—in person and online. This method is a full-circle experience, one starting with self-awareness and communication skills to identify where and when to put those skills into action. We're not focusing on logos, website messaging, or elevator pitches. Instead, we're going to delve into the "human side" of dynamic brand development by focusing on these five pillars:

B **Behavior**—Take responsibility for **your own** actions and interactions; understand that your aligned behavior leads to strong team morale and even better client retention.

R **Respect**—We'll explore ways a great leader shows respect and value for themself, their team, their brand, and their colleagues.

A **Appearance**—What is your visual signature? How do you convey confidence? In a world driven by perception, how do you need to appear, in your clothing and posture, to align with your value words and the goals of your business?

N **Networking**—A memorable Personal Brand gains strength through relationship building. There are a variety of modes in which to network: with your clients, with prospects, and an often-overlooked opportunity—with your team members who network with your clients.

D **Dynamic Dialogue**—What you say and how you say it matters deeply. How do you communicate effectively to turn leads into clients, and clients into loyal and raving fans?

Chapter 4

Behaviors That Build Your B.R.A.N.D.

Three Traits of an Intentional Leader

In the early 1990s, before I had my own business, I worked for a manager named Fred, who completely shifted my perception of what a leader should be. This short man, with dark brown, perfectly cut hair and a small pointy nose, weighed no more than a minute. What Fred lacked in height and weight, he made up for in speed and sass. He zipped around the office, checking in here and giving orders there.

When Fred joined the company, I deemed him a decent manager. Fred seemed interested when he asked me about my job, ideas for improvement in my department, and areas that I wanted to grow. His first year, I even received a lovely gold-and-silver-link choker necklace for Christmas.

Several months later, Fred paid a quick visit to my cubicle. Hunched over my keyboard, my fingers dancing over the keys as I entered a client's order, I was startled to hear my name. Fred said matter-of-factly, "I just want to let you know that Julie is now going to be your direct manager." My heart sank.

Julie, Frank's younger cousin, had joined the company nearly two years after me. My initial excited greetings and friendly smiles were met with cool brown eyes and barely upturned lips. Feeling disappointed, I resigned myself to the fact that I would not be best friends with Julie.

I had previously expressed to Fred that I'd hoped to be promoted one day. He always said, "When the time is right, we'll move you up." I could not hide the agitation in my voice when I asked, "Why Julie and not me?"

His chilly response sent me over the edge. "You don't have a college degree and Julie does." Really? How could a college degree trump a strong work ethic and job mastery? I was so much more of a demonstrated leader than Julie. Finished with his task, Fred did a quick 180-degree spin, zipped over to a colleague's cube, and casually asked how her day was going.

No emotion. No forewarning. No private discussion. No hope for my future at the company.

Was this behavior indicative of all managers? Surely not?

Any respect I had left for Fred dissipated when I made a repeat error on an order. For this conversation, at least Fred had the decency to speak with me in his office. I slowly stepped into the dimly lit room. In the middle of a wooden bookshelf sat a sweet photograph of Fred standing between two large-eyed little girls. The fluorescent lights gave Fred a ghostly glow. Turning my head, the awkward lighting revealed another unwelcome guest—Leslie, our director of finance. Leslie sat upright; her slender frame was turned slightly away. Leslie's thin lips murmured a disinterested hello. Confused and feeling ganged up on, I sat on the armchair next to Leslie. The stiff chair added to my discomfort.

Fred began by saying, "I've asked Leslie to join us today because your mistake has cost our company money." My crime?

I'd created an incorrect label for a shipment that was nearly sent to a client. Our Quality Control department discovered the issue and kindly asked me to rerun the labels correctly. Unfortunately, the mistake also required reproduction and repackaging of the shipment. I apologized and noted the correction in the file.

Leslie sat motionless, staring at Fred as if he were a Roman god. Fred continued, "We want to know how we should reprimand you. Go home tonight and think about it. Come back tomorrow with your answer." Leslie's gaze slowly shifted to me. With a wry smile and arrogant eyes, she didn't need words. Her expression said it all.

Have you ever had a manager like that? How would you feel if that were you? What would you have done?

That experience created a profound shift in my mindset of what a leader's job should be. Was it to make those in their charge feel demoralized and devalued? To lead by demanding and demeaning instructions? No way.

After a night of tears, pillow pounding, and introspection, I walked into Fred's office and saw his sidekick, Leslie, poised in her chair for my reckoning. Shaking like a leaf inside, praying my nerves did not give my planned confidence away, I said, "It's not my job to punish me, nor is it yours." I deliberately did not look to my left at Leslie. "I made a mistake for which I've already apologized to everyone. Let's talk about how the entire process can change to stop this issue from occurring again."

Fred, expecting me to grovel at his feet, sat motionless. Perplexed, he glanced over at Leslie with an "I don't know what to do next" expression. Then he looked back at me. He finally said, in a slightly softer tone, "OK. Let's schedule a follow-up meeting to review. But don't let this happen again."

Ignoring his last statement, I turned my body. With my head held high, I walked out the door, headed for the bathroom, closed the metal stall door, and let out the biggest sigh of relief.

Leadership expert and trainer Simon Sinek says, "The art of leadership is about inspiring people to build something, not threatening to break something."

Fred and Leslie tried like heck to break my spirit. They had the mindset of "demanding" attention. I've made it my life's mission to be an intentional leader who inspires those around me to know their value and "command" attention.

Leadership is a set of intentional actions or behaviors that inspire others to achieve a shared goal. In my coaching sessions, I begin my Behavior Lesson by introducing the power of taking ownership of your actions and the importance of valuing the people on your team. I demonstrate this through an acronym I call my **P.I.E. Method**.

P Teach the **PURPOSE** of the organization. When onboarding a new employee or during an annual review meeting, talk about the organization's purpose. Why does it exist? Whom do you serve? What core values are the backbone of your organization? It's critical that everyone is on the same page.

I Teach each employee their profound **IMPACT** on the success of the organization. We're not looking for department silos. Instead, a great leader consistently shares how each person is valued and how their role, from maintenance to management, is important to the success of the organization. A great leader makes decisions by thinking about both the individual employee and their impact on the entire organization.

E Lead with **EMPATHY**—In our next section, we'll explore the difference between sympathy and empathy. I can't think of a more important word than empathy in leadership or life. Connect with others; consider how they are feeling in a situation; meet your team and clients where they are; and respond verbally and nonverbally to make others feel validated and heard.

What Does It Mean to Be Present?

Today, we are a distraction-driven society. While writing, I am working on my laptop, which has two additional monitors plugged into it; my mobile phone is next to me; and my Apple watch is on my wrist, faithfully zapping every so often to remind me it's time to stand and breathe. I also have an iPad for my notes and ear buds chiming piano tunes in my ears. How much tech do you have?

To compound this frenzy, urgent emails appear like magic in our inboxes; our boss, employees, family, and clients call, text, or rap on our office doors, often expecting—or even demanding—an immediate response.

Then there is social media. How often do you find yourself sucked into this vortex?

As if that's not enough, we're still fighting the tail end of a pandemic and extreme global unrest.

With all these immense disruptions vying for your attention, how in the world can you be present for your team? Do you find yourself saying, "Hang on a second, I just got a text." Or "Sorry, I didn't hear your question, I was just finishing an email."

Distracted behavior does not go unnoticed. The more you choose to keep your eyes on your inbox or the latest text message or respond to every beep on your watch, the less valued your audience (an employee, a client, a family member) feels, and thus your credibility falters.

On the bright side, you've set aside the mayhem to read this book! If you can set aside some time for professional growth here, you can also make time for the people in your work and life.

Three behaviors epitomize the actions of an inspirational and intentional leader and demonstrate you are truly present:

- Showing empathy over sympathy
- Impeccable L.I.S.T.E.N.ing skills
- Being aware of body language

We often confuse sympathy with empathy. Sympathy is our ability to say, "I'm sorry" or "I feel bad about your situation." But the sentiment ends there. This display of remorse is fine for certain situations. However, in a business setting, when everything hinges on your behavior, you must choose empathy over sympathy.

Empathy is your ability to emotionally connect to how others are feeling. A great technique is to ask yourself, "How would I feel if I were in their shoes?" The greater the connection you demonstrate, the more your audience feels validated and heard.

A famous quote from Maya Angelou: "I've learned that people will forget what you said, people will forget what you did, but people will never forget how you made them feel."

My body shivers every time I read that quote. I love it so much!

Let's go back to my story for a minute. Did Fred show empathy toward me in either difficult situation? Did he consider speaking to me in private? Did he consider his tone of voice? Did he think his behaviors were going to motivate me to be a better team player? Not for a second. Next time you find yourself in a difficult situation, I urge you to find ways to have compassion and respect for the other person. Dignity matters.

Ask your best clients, those that have been with you for years, pay their bills on time, even give you referrals: "Why have you stayed with me for so many years?" I'm sure you'll be pleasantly surprised at the answers you receive. My favorite testimonial is: "You just get me." Yes! That's the response I want from all my clients and peers. It shows that my team and I are working hard to connect emotionally with them and demonstrate, through our service, that their needs are important to us because they are important to them.

SUCCESS EXERCISE

If your existing testimonials are old or you don't have any, stop reading and let's work on this now. Testimonials provide valuable company feedback and credibility during the sales process. Make a list of your best clients and request a testimonial!

IMPECCABLE L.I.S.T.E.N.ING SKILLS

Inevitably, every time I ask my husband, Eric, if he is listening, he furrows his brows and says, "What did you say?"

"Ha, ha, very funny," I retort.

How many jokesters do you have in your life?

While my husband and I can chuckle about his response, too many times this question is not taken seriously.

A key trait of a great leader is making a concerted effort to really ***listen*** and think about "consequences" and impact before responding. How will my response make my colleague feel? Will my response move us toward a common goal? Will my response be for the highest good of everyone? Yet how can you provide a proper response if you don't listen to what the other person is saying?

In addition to consequences, every conversation has a goal. It's important to identify and understand what that goal or desired outcome is so that you pay attention to a variety of cues and clues before initiating your response.

By actively listening, you can gather the necessary information needed to elicit the appropriate responses.

For example, you receive a call from a good client who wishes to meet. They want to provide feedback about a particular employee. Your initial response might be to think of every possible answer to questions you formulate in your head. You haven't even had the conversation; however, you are sure you know the answer.

The meeting finally arrives. Your client begins by sharing a few concerns about punctuality. You barely hear what she says, because you are so eager to blurt out your preconceived idea of what the issue could be. Hearing your response, your client looks at you with a confused expression and says she has no idea what you're talking about. Embarrassed, you blush and say, "I'm sorry. Can you repeat your issue?" Your client takes a deep breath, lets out a slow sigh, and begins again.

Has something like this happened to you? Or were you ever in your client's position? How did it make you feel? Did it stall the conversation? Did you notice an energy shift?

Think about how you can mitigate such situations. Here is a tool to guide you to become a more aware and empathetic listener.

L Look at the person you are talking to

I Interact when appropriate, but don't interrupt

S Say it back; repeat the information given

T Two-way communication

E Empathy over ego

N Nonverbal cues—body language

L—Look at the Person You Are Talking To: Eye contact is impactful. This is such a powerful component of truly demonstrating that you are interested in and value what the other person has to say. Eye contact will help you focus on them and not a side conversation in your head.

I—Interact when When Appropriate, but Don't Interrupt: Many of us have a burning need to be heard. However, the power of listening is to show you *heard* what the other person is saying. It is truly an exercise in patience. The upside: Conversations are more focused and productive when each party feels heard and the person you're speaking with sees that you're responding to the question or issue shared—versus them feeling frustrated because they were cut off.

S—Say It Back: To show you were listening and to be confident that you understood the question asked, a great strategy is to say, "To make sure I understand you, let me repeat what you just said." I love how this little bit of vulnerability confirms that you understand and were paying attention, or you need a bit more information.

T—Two-Way Communication: Listening skills always require at least a two-way conversation. Too often we forget that. It's not just one person speaking. Show respect by letting each person in your discussion speak. Be open to hearing what everyone has to say. You don't have to love it, but at least hear the other person out. To be effective, your other party should give you the same respect.

E—Empathy Over Ego: The hardest lesson of all is learning how to put your ego aside during a conversation. We are all emotional beings. Our first response is often an emotional reaction rather than a diplomatic one. Think back to your last heated conversation. What was the outcome? Did you feel the discussion was productive or counterproductive? Now, put your ego aside. Could the discussion have been less fiery if you and the other party had focused just on the facts and taken any defensive or emotional triggers out of the conversation? Did each of you maintain mutual respect?

N—Nonverbal Cues: We make all kinds of inferences based on someone's overall appearance. This includes our clothing, posture, and body language. It's important to note that "We listen with our eyes."

So, what messages are you sending? To be present, start by taking time to look professional. Looking like a "hot mess" creates a huge distraction and demonstrates a lack of respect for your brand and your colleagues. Next, become aware of your body language. Are you slouching? Rolling your eyes? Fidgeting? Pursing your lips? Each of these sends a nonverbal message. Remember intention versus interpretation here. You may intend to put your best foot forward; however, the perception or interpretation might be quite different.

Active listening is so important that we will revisit this topic throughout this book. You can start right away. Become aware of your emotion in the moment, your ego, and your body language during every conversation. Next, ask yourself, "What was the outcome of each conversation?" Did you receive any positive feedback on your communication skills or was the outcome not quite what you had hoped for? To maintain credibility and grow your brand, you must put aside your ego for a few minutes and take ownership of your behavior. If you recognize problems with active listening, take intentional steps to make positive changes.

SUCCESS TIP

It's important to check in with yourself and your actions. Self-ownership is key to maintaining self-control and credibility. Try this tip: Grab a Post-It Note or open the Notes app on your computer. Write a reminder message to yourself that says: "Empathy Over Ego." Keep this affirmation in a place where you can glance at it frequently. This is a great reminder and helpful tool when working through a variety of challenging interactions.

Emotional Intelligence—EQ Over IQ

Moment by moment, we are challenged to respond to emotional triggers. It's as if we are walking on a perpetual road, where each response we deliver allows us to take a step forward or backward—or get stuck in cement. How you and I respond to those triggers determines whether we proceed forward, go backward, or stay stuck. Forward motions are the building blocks of a strong Personal Brand.

Too often we consider technical mastery and our "IQ" to be the key foundation to building a successful business. While job aptitude is a starting point, how you make others "feel" emotionally (positive or negative) has an even larger impact on business and personal success.

The term "Emotional Intelligence," or EQ, as it is commonly abbreviated, was introduced in 1990 by researchers John Mayer and Peter Salovey. It took Daniel Goleman, then science journalist for the *New York Times*, to take Mayer and Salovey's research and bring it to a broader audience with his 1995 book, *Emotional Intelligence*. Goleman maintained that it is not just our IQ that determines success—it is our EQ.

He asserted that emotionally intelligent people had four core characteristics:

Self-Awareness—understand your own emotions	Social Awareness—understand that empathy for others drives actions
Self-Management—the ability to manage our emotions and deliver an empathetic response	Relationship Management—the ability to navigate and respond empathetically to the various emotions in a group

In this section, you will learn key strategies for building credibility with others by being present. We do this by incorporating EQ in every conversation we have to create meaningful interactions.

EQ always begins with self-awareness.

- How does the situation I am in make me feel?
- What emotions are stirring inside of me?
- How I can harness my feelings or calm myself down so that I manage my emotions, respond with integrity, and am empathetic toward how others are feeling?

I know, easier said than done! EQ essentially needs to be at the forefront of every discussion you have and assessed before each response you deliver.

If that's not hard enough, you also need to consider social intelligence. Who is in your group and how do you manage your response in order to add value, have a positive influence, and increase credibility?

Start by assessing who is in the audience, group discussion, or even on your team.

Next, understand that each person is very different from you. I am totally asking you to jump out of your "well" and consider each person's job knowledge, education, role in their organization, cultural upbringing, and unique set of values. Each of these traits will be subliminally summoned each time an emotional response is required.

Finally, after gauging your group's structure, share your response or feedback in a tone of voice that brings the group harmony and clarity. Take care not to sound or appear (nonverbal behavior) insensitive, unfeeling, or frustrated. This will only splash you right back in the bottom of your well. You'll have to work extra hard to earn trust back and climb back out.

Lisa's Shorr-to-Shine Time Management Strategies

In 2019, my husband and I had the amazing opportunity to learn from Dr. Nido Qubein at North Carolina's High Point University, where he has been president since 2005. Dr. Qubein immigrated to America with his mother from Lebanon as a teenager. Acclimation to their new home proved tricky. They had limited knowledge of the English language and culture, and they had only $50 to their name.

Dr. Qubein's mother was a driving force in his life, and he proudly shared his mother's wisdom throughout our two-day seminar. Early in his training, he shared a powerful quote: "It's OK to be disappointed, just not discouraged." He said to never let setbacks hold you back—learn from them and keep pushing.

When Eric, my colleagues, and I arrived on campus, we were instantly impressed by the manicured landscaping and spouting water fountains all around campus. Our classroom was not typical either. We didn't feel wedged between a tiny desk with an attached metal seat. Our class was held in a lecture hall with comfortable desk chairs with wide mesh backs that swiveled from side to side. The back wall was made entirely of glass, as were those of many classrooms. This made the school feel more open and collaborative. A large modern whiteboard was flanked on either side by two majestic American flags. A projector screen slowly emerged from the ceiling to display his slides. Such an inspiring environment in which to learn!

Dr. Qubein's list of accomplishments is long. President of High Point University, executive chairman of the Great Harvest Bread Company, corporate board member of several Fortune 500 companies, and author and keynote speaker (just to name a few).

Hoping to garner the secret to Dr. Qubein's success, one of my colleagues raised her hand and asked, "With all that you do, how do you manage your time?"

His response was quick and confident. "I don't manage my time; I manage my energy." He went on to share that he values his time and sets priorities for his day. He first asks:

- What can I control?
- What is out of my control?
- What can I delegate?
- What activities can wait?
- What can I make more efficient?

He went on to share that if you're unsure what to prioritize, it's important to take a "recess to reassess your business." You owe it to your clients, employees, and most importantly, yourself.

SUCCESS EXERCISE

It's time to take a short recess from your business to look at how you spend your day. I want you to be productive and maximize your time.

Let's explore eight areas in your business where you can either improve processes or delegate tasks, thus freeing up your time to focus on building your business. Answer the following questions below.

Do you:

1. Document and share S.M.A.R.T. Goals so that you make decisions that align with your goals—rather than busying yourself with activities that have no real clarity around whether each is is a needed task? *Note: Rewrite your S.M.A.R.T. Goals from Chapter 2 here. Next, share them with your team to ensure decisions and tasks align with goal achievement.*
2. Have a documented process for each area of your business to standardize procedures to allow autonomy of your employees so they don't have to constantly come to you for help? *Note: List the procedures you need to standardize first. Ideas could include onboarding a new client, onboarding a new employee, or answering the phones.*
3. Have copious notes from each meeting you can easily share with your team members and add to your client file? *Note: There are several options including online note takers, transcriptions from recording a meeting, and more. How can you improve your note taking and sharing?*
4. Abdicate or ignore company or department projects? It's important to trust, but critical to inspect progress along the way. *Note: If ignoring, list projects you now need to check on:*
5. Block off time in your calendar for meetings and project work? Or do you wing it every day and just react when the phone rings? *Note: Value your time. Lack of preparation/time hurts brand credibility. Schedule all meetings and create a standard agenda. For projects, create a standard process from kickoff to completion.*

Do you:

6.	Have short daily (or at least weekly) meetings to check in on the team with clear meeting agendas and strict time schedules? A huge time waster is starting on one topic, getting offtrack, then realizing you're out of time and need to set a new meeting to finish your agenda. *Note: Create a standard agenda template to follow.*
7.	Regularly assess what can be improved or automated in your business or department? Examples include adding a client payment portal, so you don't rely on snail mail to receive checks or automating a series of marketing emails to share news and tips to your client and prospect list. *Note: Make a list of three areas to automate in your business.*
8.	Schedule time for social media posting and surfing? Better yet, can you delegate it to an employee? *Notes: Start now! Write 3–5 social media post ideas.*

The more you identify and focus on your priorities, the more present and attentive you can be to listen to employee needs, build client relationships, and strategically grow your business. Becoming a master of your time and managing your energy makes this possible.

CHAPTER 5

DEMONSTRATING RESPECT

Marcus Lemonis, TV personality and CEO of Camping World, World, stood in the middle of 1,100 small IT business owners. Instead of keynoting from the stage, Marcus chose to present eye-to-eye with his audience. He dressed in a fitted, solid white, cable-knit crew neck sweater, slim fit faded jeans, and stylish sneakers. His short hair was perfectly cut and his smile was genuine.

He started his keynote by paying homage to the IT industry for keeping businesses cyber safe. My peers and I cheered in gratitude.

He then shifted the conversation and probed the audience: "What is one bad habit you stopped doing during Covid?" and "What is one new habit you started during Covid?"

He asked us to dig deep and tap into our emotions. Most of us caught on quick that if you made eye contact with Marcus, he was going to call on you to stand up and share. Unfortunately, my colleague Joe, sitting at the round table next to mine, didn't shift his gaze away from Marcus quick enough!

With an outstretched arm, Marcus pointed right at him. "You, over there in the beige T-shirt, come on up and let's talk." After a bit of prodding, a reluctant Joe sauntered to the middle of the audience next to Marcus, who asked, "What's your issue?"

Joe had a serious look on his face. Already feeling vulnerable, he shared, "I'm angry."

Marcus probed further. What was he angry about? Joe looked down. His body seemed frozen. Silence spread through the large conference room. All we could hear was the breath emanating from Marcus's microphone.

Finally, Joe replied, "With me for not pushing myself."

Delving deeper, Marcus got Joe to divulge that his anger was being taken out on his employees. Now he was getting to the root of the issue.

Joe shared that he felt like he wasn't pushing himself hard enough, which was impacting his personal and professional life. The anger he was feeling was being displaced onto his team members.

At this point, Marcus could have judged my colleague and labeled him a bad leader. Instead, he displayed immense respect for Joe's candor and acknowledged that many people feel the same.

Before he allowed Joe to scurry back to his table, Marcus shared one last bit of advice: "You need to look for your weaknesses and ask yourself—what can you do better? How do you get your act together? Home life is the foundation to success in the rest of your life. Start there."

Pondering this experience, I realized that Marcus was asking Joe to take ownership of and respect for where he was in his career. Next step, determine what could he do to change his outlook and actions.

Marcus Lemonis said he cared more about EQ (emotional intelligence) than IQ. Tears of empathy for Joe and validation for the work that I do trickled down my face. That powerful exchange made me understand that there are three ways to demonstrate respect:

1. For yourself
2. For others
3. For your Corporate Brand

Let's explore each.

You've Got to Take Time for You—Ideas for Self-Care

On Marcus Lemonis's website, I read a quote: "*People respect you more if they get the truth as opposed to a bunch of fluff.*"

What is your "fluff?" What stories do you tell yourself as to why you can't take care of yourself? Take that vacation? Grow your business? Or "Why it's OK to take your frustrations out on someone else?"

You have so many gifts that brought you to where you are today. Start by appreciating the following:

- **The gift of your personal values**—Refer back to your value words. Read them again. They are special and unique to you. Use them to drive your personal success as a foundation to drive others forward as well.
- **The gift of your knowledge**—Erase the belief that you must know everything to be successful. You sure don't. I struggled for many years thinking I was "an imposter" because I was "not technical" in my technology business. My brain would twist whenever Eric talked to my engineers about a client's computer network issue.

I felt like a ship begging to explore the ocean, but for many years shame and a limiting sense of confidence were anchors holding me back. I needed to dislodge the anchors and to understand and respect my unique gifts of creative writing, brand building, and empathy. As the chief marketer in my company, it was and is my job to promote our tech services in a nontechnical way to attract new business. It was not my job to physically fix anything. Once I understood that, my anchor was lifted, and I set sail and experienced greater success.

Sit for a moment and answer: What are your unique skills? List the special skills and talents you possess. Are you mechanical, analytical, creative, empathetic? Now smile and appreciate those skills. I am proud of you!

- **The gift of your experiences**—What life experiences brought you to where you are today? Do you view them as traumas or triumphs? Is each experience meant to teach you a lesson? Teach someone else a lesson? Or create a paradigm shift in your industry, community, or even across the globe?

  This is no easy feat. It's best accomplished by surrounding yourself with positive, supportive people.

SUCCESS EXERCISE

Make a list of the people in your life who can help you appreciate your experiences and compassionately support your growth in a profound way.

- **The gift of your personality**—No one is you—and you are amazing! Don't get lost wishing you were more like anyone else. They are on their own journey. You are perfect the way you are!

One more wise ancient quote that inspires me is *"Respect yourself and others will respect you."*—Confucius. A perfect starting point. Once our personal house is in order, we can then **be present** for others.

If you are giving me pushback right now, I get it. You have a million items on your to-do list and there is not enough room for self-care. I created this list of strategies to respect you, the busy business owner. Some are meant to be applied during the workday; others are meant to encourage you to take a break from working altogether.

SEVEN SUCCESS STRATEGIES

1. **Lisa's 4 x 4 x 4 Breathing Method**—We've all heard the phrase "Calm down, take a deep breath." There is true merit in this statement. A respected leader has the capacity to maintain their cool in stressful situations. It's critical to stop and listen to your body and take measures to self-soothe to gain self-control. Practice this breathing exercise to encourage ease of effective communication.

Follow these steps:

- **Step 1**: Take a deep breath by inhaling through your nose for 4 seconds.
- **Step 2**: Now slowly exhale through your mouth for 4 seconds.

- **Step 3**: Repeat steps 1 and 2 four times. Note: Feel free to do this exercise as many times as you need; four is a great baseline.

2. **Meditation**—Many leaders find solace, focus, and reduced anxiety levels when they calm their mind through regular meditation. Try meditating in conjunction with focused breathing to boost your mood, reduce stress, improve focus, and more. If, like me, you struggle with independent meditating, no worries. There are a ton of videos online—from five minutes to one hour—to help you. Find one you connect with.

3. **Desk Exercises**—Even if your day is jam-packed, some form of exercise each day will help keep your blood flowing, stretch stiff sedentary muscles, and help with posture. There is a plethora of online videos to pick from.
   - Keep small 3- to 5-pound hand weights at your desk to work your arms, shoulders, triceps, and upper back.
   - Resistance bands—I love using my bands to stretch my often-tense neck muscles. They're also great for loosening tight hips and thighs, and for doing chest presses and triceps extensions.
   - Chair yoga—Stretch, stretch, and stretch some more.

4. **Hydrate With Water**—There are so many adverse effects of dehydration. Among them are a foggy mind, dizziness, and feeling physically weak. How can you possibly lead your organization in this state? Make a concerted effort to always have water with you. It'll keep you alert, honor

your internal body, and support vocal stamina by keeping your vocal cords moist. We need our voices to share our ideas and inspiration.

5. **Step Away From the Situation**—If you're in a situation that will cause you to act in a way that's not in alignment with your value words, or hinders your ability to maintain credibility as a leader, step away. Not every situation must be resolved immediately. Many successful negotiations occur after each party has had time to think rationally versus feeling pressured or bullied. If you feel uncomfortable, say to the person, "I'd like to resume this conversation later. I'd like to do more research or take some time to calm myself down." Respect your credibility and the credibility of your business.

6. **Vacation**—What more can I say here? Taking the time to unplug and unwind will always help you recharge your batteries. If a full week isn't possible, aim for a weekend getaway instead.

7. **Hobbies**—What do you do for fun? What fulfills you? Gardening, cooking, reading, journaling, running, biking, volunteering for a nonprofit organization? The key is to find a hobby that doesn't necessarily reflect your day-to-day work. Hobbies have the amazing benefits of showcasing our additional strengths, sparking feelings of satisfaction or accomplishment, helping us heal from difficult experiences, decreasing anxiety, providing physical activity, and so much more.

SUCCESS EXERCISE

Honor yourself! Make a list of activities you'll start today that will respect your needs and drive you forward. I'll get you started with a S.M.A.R.T. Goal example: Drank 6–8 glasses of water by the end of every day. What is next on your list?

Actions of a Leadership S.T.A.R.

When my eldest daughter was around 18 months old, she started showing interest in potty training. I was so excited about the possibility of saving money and having one less child (she has a younger sister) in diapers.

Not wanting to lose momentum, I drove to my local drug store and purchased a large piece of construction paper and a package of shiny stars. I sat with my daughter and created a fun chart. Every time she successfully used the potty, she would earn a star. She even got to pick the color. When she completed a row, she got a fun size bag of M&M's. You might call this bribery; I call it an early stage "incentive plan."

When I became a business owner, I thought about how to earn my "stars" and gain respect and credibility as a leader from my employees and colleagues. I lovingly remembered my days potty training my first daughter and how my husband and I cheered her on and rewarded her for efforts and successes along the way.

While training my daughter lasted only a few short months, a respected business owner or manager must work on earning their stars every single day. A Leadership S.T.A.R., as I lovingly call you, acknowledges and values not just their own Personal Brand, but spends even more time building the brands of their team members and seeking ways to enhance their Corporate Brand. Here are four areas that will help you to earn your S.T.A.R.:

S Show Empathy

T Take Time for You

A Appreciate Your Corporate Brand

R Research and Review Your Business

S—Show Empathy—I will continue to mention empathy multiple times throughout this book. Find ways to connect emotionally to others. Make a concerted effort to put yourself in others' shoes. Show you care by asking validating questions, such as "So I better understand, can you tell me more about how you feel?" Demonstrate actions that show you are trying to share in an emotion or taking action to help resolve a problem.

T—Take Time for You—I intentionally started this chapter with ways to take time for you. As Marcus Lemonis alluded to our group, we've got to take care of ourselves first. Respect your mental and physical state. We can't be great leaders if we are in less-than-optimal health. Period. Now, go grab some water, do a five-minute stretch, and come on back to read on!

A—Appreciate Your Corporate Brand—Too often we confuse our Corporate Brand with our logo and website. Those are two important aspects, yet our brand is so much more than that. It's our culture, core values, client testimonials, processes and cross-training within each department, our dress standards, communication between departments, and even the condition of our physical office space. All these aspects and more contribute to the experience that you, your employees, clients, and prospects have on a day-to-day basis.

Take stock of your entire office. What do you see? What can you change? Ask your employees for their feedback and ideas on how to make your environment even better and more collaborative. How can you enhance client experience? **Note**: Set your ego aside and just LISTEN to ideas and see what you can honor and what you are unable to accommodate.

R—Research and Review Your Business—An often-overlooked strategy to build your brand and maintain "S.T.A.R." status focuses on paying attention to the details. My two Rs to implement this are "research" and "review."

Research—Research means you are putting the extra effort into learning more. I always begin my first interview with a candidate with *"Tell me, what do you know about me and my company?"* Inevitably, the candidate sheepishly shrugs his or her shoulders and says something like, "I didn't have time to research you before this call." This drives me nuts and is an instant red flag. I want the candidate to show me that they took the extra step and are on this call because they respect the brand and are excited about the opportunity to be a contributor to its growth.

How does doing research ahead of time show respect? Since perception is reality, the more research you do and questions you prepare, the greater chance you will be perceived as being detail-oriented, along with honoring and admiring both your brand and theirs.

The goal is to be perceived by employees, clients, and potential clients as proactive versus reactive. How many of these areas do you research consistently?

Do you:

- Spend time researching new client projects by first reviewing similar projects previously completed. What went well? What needs adjustment? Did you make a profit?
- Spend time researching more innovative ways to serve your clients?
- Spend time pulling together questions and documentation to review during a client meeting?
- Research and test new products internally before deploying them to your clients?
- Look up directions and confirm appointments ahead of time?
- Set proper "impact and time expectations" with clients during project implementations?
- Research and deal with client issues immediately, or do you procrastinate?

What else would you add to this list?

Review—Complacency is a brand and credibility crusher. When we are complacent, we stop making improvements.

Chet Holmes, late author of the book ***The Ultimate Sales Machine***, said, "People respect what you inspect." A brand cannot maintain its status when you don't hold yourself and others accountable.

As a small business owner, you wear many hats. You are busy running around serving clients, ordering products, and sending out invoices. You are so busy being reactive that you don't make time for growth activities. A great example: not consistently reviewing your company metrics. When was the last time you looked at your receivables? How about your net profits? Have you ever been faced with a cash-flow conundrum and wished you had raised prices sooner or stayed on top of collections more frequently?

There are many areas to review to ensure brand sustainability and growth. I suggest you start here:

- **Branding Everywhere**—Is your current logo on your website, invoices, wrapped vehicles, office walls? Don't confuse others by having two different logos for your organization.

- **Dress Standards**—Your team is a physical extension of your brand. The way they appear could directly correlate to assumptions about the type of work they will produce. We'll talk more about this in the next chapter.

- **Phone Skills**—Phone etiquette is vital! The phones often create a "first impression" of your business. How does your team sound when on the phone? What are they saying to your clients? Do you have **a documented process** for handling leads that call into your office? Is this process being used, or is each employee given the freedom to say what they want? Don't jump ahead, but I am dedicating Chapter 9 to Polishing Your Phone Skills.

- **Condition of Your Desks and Office**—Yes, this is on this list, especially since many of us have hybrid offices. An unkempt desk or office can easily be a distraction if you are on a virtual call. It sends the perceived message that if your office is sloppy your work will be too. Imagine you have a new client coming to visit your office. What do you want them to see and think?

- **Virtual Appearance**—Today's dress standards have relaxed. That doesn't mean we don't have to care about how we appear. In a virtual meeting, we have such a small window, literally, to impress our audience. We want to appear professional and in alignment with our brand.

- **Quality of Projects and Day-to-Day Work**—Don't assume the work is getting done to your standards if you don't have a regular process in place to spot-check and oversee work in a consistent manner. This does not mean you should micromanage. However, when an employee knows that their work will be closely reviewed, they will put more effort into quality and outcomes. You don't want to have the dangerous mindset of "we've always done it this way."

- **Your Attitude**—Check this one daily! Your attitude sets the tone for your outlook for the day, as well as how you will interact with your peers. Culture and morale start at the top—with you. Take time to take care of you, your wellness, and your attitude at your office.

- **Your Metrics**—Don't wait to meet with your CPA just for tax planning. Set quarterly meetings. Additionally, sales numbers, including leads into your office, sales closed, and pending quotes—to name a few—should be reviewed weekly. Compare all these numbers against the goals you've set for your business. A lack of follow-up is a huge revenue loser!

SUCCESS EXERCISE

Sit down and create a few meetings in your calendar. A weekly reoccurring sales and marketing meeting, monthly corporate numbers meeting (to review P&L statements and the balance sheet), a monthly collections meeting, and a quarterly tax planning meeting with your CPA. This is a good starting point to have a much keener eye on the revenue coming into and going out of your business.

Can You Lead With Lollipops?

One evening, my daughter (who was fifteen at the time and is now twenty) and I were chatting about a Youth Group event she had just attended. With dancing eyes and an excited tone, she shared the theme of the event, which was leadership. I instantly perked up.

She said, "Mom, my group leader thinks like you! *He thinks that each one of us has a responsibility to take a leadership role in making our group and the world a better place.*"

I smiled, feeling validated and excited to learn that my daughter had truly listened to me. I encouraged her to tell me more.

She said, "We just watched a cool TED Talk that I know you'll like. It's called 'Leading with Lollipops.'"

She knows me well!

Watching the talk, I was engrossed from the moment Drew Dudley asked his audience, "How many of you are completely comfortable with calling yourselves a leader?" He went on to say that "We've made leadership about something bigger than us, beyond us. We made it about changing the world."

With humor, he goes on to share a profound story about how he was bouncing around a bustling college campus of incoming freshmen, handing out lollipops while promoting a nonprofit organization. At a pivotal moment, when one young freshman girl was about to step out of the registration line, head for home, and scrap her college plans, Drew Dudley jovially appeared.

He handed a lollipop to a shy boy standing next to the girl and said, *"Give this lollipop to the beautiful woman standing next to you."* Dudley reenacted the motion of the embarrassed boy extending his arm and looking down, red-faced, handing the lollipop to the girl. The crowd around them roared. Dudley was about to move to the next group but first looked seriously at the girl's parents and said, *"Look at that. Look at that. First day away from home and she is already taking candy from a stranger."* That moment would change the trajectory of each of those unassuming student's lives. The best part of that story is that one act of kindness led to not only the girl staying in college, but eventually marrying that embarrassed boy. Even more interesting, Dudley didn't even remember the event. The female student reminded him of it four years later. Wow. This is a must-watch TEDx Talk.

Lollipop moments are not just events that happen to you and me, they're the seemingly small but impactful events that have a profound impact on others.

Like Drew Dudley, I've always believed that when we think of the term "Leader," we make it a bigger, more aspirational term than it should be. I believe that each person in an organization, no matter their level or title, is a leader—a leader of their own job and career path.

Some folks in an organization have more responsibility than others. Each of us, however, has a direct impact on the outcome of the organization. Marketing brings in the leads to your sales department. Sales signs new deals or upsells deals with existing clients that the procurement department orders. Your service and account management teams have a direct impact on accounts payable and receivable. The CEO or owner is responsible for the organization's overall energy and flow. Each is interdependent of the other and should be respected as equally important.

I remember a conversation I had with one of my engineers about buying a house. He said "one day" he'd like to figure out how to buy a house. I was determined to help him make his dream a reality. We talked about setting goals. Using the same strategies mentioned earlier in this book, we created a S.M.A.R.T. Goal to have a house under contract by May of the following year. We then talked about actions to take to achieve that goal.

I am proud to share that this goal became a reality! Not only did he sign the contract, he's now building another house. I love seeing my team members succeed. I felt so gratified when I got this email: *"Lisa, when you helped me to pick a specific date to be prequalified, I was scared. But I get it 100%. Being specific and intentional with goals and dreams makes a difference. Every day I must CHOOSE to be intentional with my attitude and mindset."*

Are you asking what this story has to do with respect? A leader has admiration and respect for others' well-being and growth. We will do what we can to see those around us succeed, even if we don't know who they are. We don't try to hoard all the accolades for ourselves. Our brand and credibility grow when we unselfishly support those in our family, workplace, and community at large.

You never know when a simple lollipop moment will shift the life of a stranger.

SUCCESS EXERCISE

Ask your team to share stories of lollipop moments that profoundly impacted them—or others.

CHAPTER 6

Busting the Myth That Appearance Doesn't Matter

Filled with excitement, my husband and I scurried around, tidying up and cleaning our kitchen. We cleared and cleaned dated dark brown countertops and stacked plates into equally dated forty-year-old wooden cabinets. Natural cracks and crevices peppered the stone floors. Even worse, our cabinet configuration was unsightly. One set protruded from the wall over a countertop in an "L" formation. Ironically, this was where our guests congregated. While I hoped they'd remember my entertaining with lovely food and conversation, inevitability, they remembered banging their heads on the cabinet while reaching for a slice of cheese off a beautiful crudité platter.

For nearly ten years, we "made do" with this kitchen and all its faults. Finally, our refrigerator conked out and we decided to commit to upgrading our kitchen.

The doorbell rang with a startling ding-dong! Smiling, I excitedly opened the door. In front of me stood a young woman dressed in skinny jeans, sandals, and a too tight V-neck sweater that exposed a bit too much skin. The young man next to her looked as if he'd just finished painting a house. He wore khaki cargo shorts, a worn gray T-shirt with the Nike logo prominently displayed across his chest, and coordinating Nike sneakers. Well-worn socks peeked out around his ankles, appearing faded and light gray from being washed with other colors too many times.

My eyes must have revealed my confusion; I was somewhat taken aback by the two people in front of me. The young woman enthusiastically introduced herself and her partner. "Hi, I'm Barbara," she said. "I'll be your lead kitchen designer, and this is Tim, my design intern."

"Hi," I said. "Welcome to my home. Come on in and let me show you what you've got work with." I tried saying this in a joking tone, hoping my initial facial reaction wasn't going to set the tone for our first meeting.

Barbara bustled around my kitchen, confidently extending her bright yellow measuring tape across the cabinets and countertops, calling out a variety of dimensions to Tim, who carefully wrote each one with his sharpened #2 pencil on an 8½" x 11" yellow notepad.

Barbara and Tim showed up intending to be perceived as professional and detail-oriented. My and my husband's interpretation was anything but. Thankfully, they redeemed themselves with professional behavior and demonstrated competence in taking measurements and providing initial design ideas.

We decided to let their appearance slide in favor of technical know-how—until visit number two. This time, Barbara arrived alone to take a few additional measurements. Once again, she rang our doorbell and greeted me with a warm smile. A quick survey of her "work attire" revealed a lovely soft beige crew neck sweater paired with a short plaid miniskirt. I felt panicked. What was she going to measure? Was she going to crawl on my floor or climb on my stepstool in that skirt?

Barbara confidently assured me that this new set of measurements would take only a few minutes. Then she awkwardly got down on my kitchen floor while shifting and tugging at her skirt to make sure nothing was exposed. After grabbing the additional data she needed, she placed one hand on the bottom of her skirt, as if holding it down for dear life, while the other was on my kitchen counter helping her balance and rise gracefully. She thanked me for the time and made her way back to the office.

After she left, I thought, *Whew! Fashion crisis averted.* Instead of being excited for my new kitchen, I was worried about Barbara's Personal Brand and that of the design company.

I decided to book a meeting with Kate, the design company's owner. We'd been business colleagues for several years; I knew we could have a productive discussion.

After a quick welcome hug, I told Kate how excited Eric and I were to have our kitchen transformed and we were looking forward to seeing Barbara's design options. Kate replied with a proud smile and an excited "Me too."

Kate's smiling face turned somber when I shifted the conversation and shared my perception of Barbara's appearance. Knowing I was an image consultant, she took what I had to say seriously. I explained, "You sell a very high-end product. Your client could be spending anywhere from five to six figures with you, depending on the size of their project. Your design team should align with your luxury brand, especially since they are the first impression of your business and your primary salespeople."

Kate dropped her eyes and let out a small sigh. "You're not the first person to tell me this. In fact, I've received similar feedback about a few other designers as well. I never like receiving calls like that. I've just never known how to properly relay the feedback to my team."

After a few more minutes of discussion, we agreed that we would partner together—I'd provide a series of workshops on the power of a first impression, help create and introduce a company-wide dress code policy, and offer a framework for a capsule wardrobe (a selection of timeless clothing with pieces that mix and match to create several outfits).

Does What You Wear Really Matter?

The answer to this question is a resounding YES! While I love to talk about the latest style and fashion trends, that's not the point of this chapter. The "A" in my B.R.A.N.D. Method is all about the power and influence a professional appearance has when creating the image of a strong leader.

There are two primary reasons why what you wear matters.

1. The Leader Sets the Culture

> Oxford Learner's Dictionaries defines image as *"The impression that a person, an organization, or a product, etc. gives to the public."*
>
> During my coaching sessions, I say that we are all a walking "billboard" for the goods and services we represent. Your image directly impacts how the public perceives you.

As we discussed earlier, we all have different sets of values. We use those principles to make "value judgments" based on our previous experiences.

As a leader, you have the primary responsibility to set the tone and expectations for the entire company. An unkempt leader begets unkempt employees, which then begets the potential perception that the work produced will be disorganized as well.

Maybe you're thinking, *My company is so casual. Do I really need to care about what I or my team wears*? Think of it this way—if you're standing next to your competitor dressed in shorts, a T-shirt, and sneakers, and he or she is dressed in a nice shirt, dress pants, and stylish shoes, whom do you think your clients will perceive as more competent and professional? Most likely it will be your competitor. Remember, we're talking about how the public perceives you and remembers you, not what you are most comfortable in.

2. Clothing Influences How You Feel

Think back to a time when you prepared for a big meeting. Was it a job interview? Making a sales pitch to your largest-ever prospect? Maybe it was delivering a keynote presentation to a large audience. To prepare for the big moment, you spent hours writing notes and practicing what you were going to say. I bet you also spent equal time deciding what you were going to wear, selecting the perfect outfit that would make you look credible and feel powerful.

When I was in sixth grade, I had a teal and white horizontal striped short-sleeved shirt with matching teal pants with a thin white stripe running down either side of my legs. I loved how the coordinated outfit made me feel put-together and gave the impression (so I thought) of someone who paid attention to detail. I have carried this love of a coordinated outfit over 40 years later! Heck, it's even become a key component of this book and my coaching program.

In 2012, researchers Hajo Adam and Adam Galinsky from Northwestern University's Kellogg School of Management wanted to see how clothing induced performance-based behavior when it had a symbolic meaning. They called this phenomenon "enclothed cognition." They ran a series of tests using a "white lab coat as the premise." One group was told to wear the coat and perceive themselves as a doctor. Another was told to wear the coat and perceive themselves as a painter, while a third group was told to perform the tests while just looking at the lab coat and thinking it was for a doctor.

The studies revealed that those wearing the coat and thinking they were a doctor outperformed groups from all other scenarios. The results showed that when clothing is assigned symbolic meaning to the person wearing it, it has psychological influence on performance.

So the next time you're getting ready for a big event and want the audience to perceive you as confident and credible, consider what you are going to wear. In the next section, you'll learn how to do this.

How Do You Build a Professional Wardrobe?

How do you apply the concept of enclothed cognition into your workday? Like corporate goals, I suggest you apply "fashion goals" too. Alyce Parsons, founder of the Universal Style system and a pioneer in the image consulting industry, shared three questions to ask when preparing for your day. The first two have an external impact and the third has an internal impact.

1. What do you want your clothing to do for you? (External Impact)

2. What do you want your clothing to say about you? (External Impact)

3. What power do you want your clothing to give you? (Internal Impact)

What do you want your clothing to do for you?
What purpose do you want your clothing to play that day? Do you have an interview? A meeting in front of your board? Each experience aligns with different clothing styles, colors, and even the fabrics you select.

What do you want your clothing to say about you?
Do you want to be perceived as prepared? Professional? Detail-oriented? As an image professional, I make it a point to always consider how I want to be perceived by everyone I encounter. I want to be seen as "put together" and "stylish"—as someone who understands how to dress for all occasions. Many prospects become clients because they say to me, "You always look so put together and confident. How do I do that?" That comes from making intentional choices about what I am wearing based on who my audience is that day.

What power do you want your clothing to give you?
Think enclothed cognition here. Does the item you are selecting make you feel confident, authoritative, knowledgeable?

There are many great reasons companies incorporate dress codes into their workplaces. Uniforms offer a sense of pride and belonging. Studies have also shown that when we get "dressed up" our mindset shifts, and we become more alert and productive in our workday.

The next time you're standing in front of your closet selecting an outfit, don't just pull anything out. First, think back to Chapter 3 and the three value words you chose to represent you. Does your clothing align with each word?

Next, consider the three questions above. Do you need your outfit to show your creativity? Your pride in your Corporate Brand? That you're an expert in your field?

Your outfit does not have to stop with clothing. Accessories can have a dramatic effect on your behavior and energy. Go ahead, put on those fabulous shoes that make you walk with confidence or that fancy watch that gives you "timeless" energy.

The Leader's Closet—Building a Capsule Wardrobe

When I mention Facebook founder Mark Zuckerberg, what is the first visual you have of him? The infamous "gray hoodie" sweatshirt over a simple crew neck T-shirt and faded jeans? That was "his signature look" until 2018 when he was called to testify in front of Congress regarding Facebook's privacy issues. Google this, and you'll see Mark in a tailored navy jacket, crisp white Oxford shirt, and light blue tie.

Either he knew the appropriate dress to wear when addressing Congress or he hired an Image Consultant to guide him. The dress code for Congress, while a bit more relaxed in recent years, is still very conservative. The lesson here? It's imperative to do some audience analysis and dress for the industry you are addressing.

Your professional wardrobe does not have to encompass a rack of tailored navy and gray suits. Nor should it consist solely of hooded sweatshirts. All you need are a few key pieces that can be interchangeable and can either be dressed up or down, depending on the occasion. This mix-and-match wardrobe is called a *capsule wardrobe.*

The beauty of a capsule wardrobe is that it can be an efficient tool for getting dressed in the morning. It can also be cost-effective when shopping because you will buy pieces that align with the capsule—versus random items that don't match and will hang in your closet with the tags still on them for the next five years.

FOUR GUIDING PRINCIPLES OF A CAPSULE WARDROBE

To help you put your capsule together, consider these four principles:

- **Principle #1: Keep Your Core Color Spectrum Neutral**—Start by adding solid neutral toned pants, tops, and jackets in white, beige, navy, gray, camel, khaki, chocolate brown, and black. Also add dark denim jeans. These will act as your base tones for building your wardrobe. Next, coordinate these items with accent colors, prints, and patterns. These principles apply for both men and women.

  For example, take your beige pants and pair them with a pin-striped blouse (women) or button-down Oxford shirt (men). Your beige pants can also be paired with a fun sweater with horizontal stripes. Or you can have a solid blue shirt/blouse paired with pinstriped pants. You may also pair your blue blouse or Oxford shirt with dark denim jeans, without rips or frays. (Style Tip: Dark denim is perceived as the most professional of all denim washes.). The key is to have a neutral tone anchor the outfit.

- **Principle #2: Congruent Story**—All the pieces in your capsule wardrobe should align with your Corporate Brand and tell one professional, harmonious story. We don't want to wear nice pants and shoes and pair them with an old concert T-shirt with a band logo blazing across your chest. Unless you are in the music industry, this is not a look that says *I am aligning with my Corporate Brand*; it may confuse or distract your audience.
- **Principle #3: Select Compatible Fabrics**—Some fabrics hold more perceived authority than others. Merino wool, cotton, silk, and certain polyester blends send a much more professional message than a thick cable knit sweater, corduroy, or linen. So when putting your capsules together for work, consider which fabrics will coordinate with the most pieces to send your desired visual message.
- **Principal #4: Align Your Accessories**—Here's where the fun comes in!
    - Men—you've got watches, socks, belts, and pocket squares for your blazers, to name a few.
    - Ladies—we have even more to choose from! Scarves, pashmina wraps, necklaces, earrings, bracelets, belts, shoes! I could write a book solely on the power of accessories.

When we are thinking about our capsules, be sure the accessories complement your look and express your personality. They are meant to create the "mood" of your look. The accessories you wear to a business meeting will differ from those worn to a fancy dinner party.

How to Build Your Capsule Collection—Men

Visualize an organization chart. The top of the chart is the CEO/Owner. In the next row are the organization's senior vice presidents. Below that are the department managers and finally, the support staff.

Now, visualize each of those rows once again. This time, instead of visualizing a person, I want you to shift to clothing. It'll look like this:

- **CEO Level—Investment Pieces**. One gray or navy suit and one navy sport coat. The suit, while not worn as often as the other pieces, is a must-have. You want to be prepared for that big meeting! If a suit really is not your thing, at least have one to two tailored sport coats to dress up your look when you need to. This is especially important if your client base is in a more conservatively dressed industry such as legal, banking, or financial.
- **Senior Vice Presidents—High-Quality Slacks/Pants**. I recommend having four to five pair—charcoal, navy, black, khaki, and dark denim jeans. These will be the base of your day-to-day wardrobe, so I recommend spending a little more on quality and take care when laundering them to lengthen their life.
- **Managers—Shirts and Sweaters**. I recommend a combination of button-down Oxford shirts in white, light blue, light purple, even pinstripe. Add in some polo shirts, cotton blend shirts, and dress T-shirts. Also include a couple of nice wool V-neck, crew, or zip-front sweaters for colder days. Don't forget the crisp white T-shirt

to go under your shirts to smooth out chest hair and absorb sweat.

- **Support Staff—The Accessories.** This is really where your personality shines. Lace-up or loafer-style brown and black shoes and one other dressy leather or vegan leather shoe. (Note: I didn't mention gym sneakers. I'm specifically talking about your office attire, not what to wear to the gym.) Coordinating brown and black belts always look sharp, along with a nice watch and high-quality briefcase or computer bag. A fun pop of interest when wearing a sport coat is a pocket square. This is a small, usually square piece of material that peeks out of the top pocket next to your lapel. There are a variety of patterns and colors that would add that extra bit of excitement to your look. Have fun with them!

How to Build Your Capsule Collection—Women

All right, ladies, let's have some fun. I'm going to use the same tiered chart for you.

- **CEO Level—Investment Pieces.** In the past I would suggest a formal suit consisting of a matching blazer and skirt or smart-looking dress with jacket. We have become a much more casual society, so I now recommend one nice navy, gray, or other coordinating pantsuit. Also, add in one or two other good blazers. These blazers could be in a pattern or other color that energizes you. Just remember to make sure they align with several other items in your capsule wardrobe.

- **Senior Vice Presidents—High-Quality Slacks/Pants.** Next, add three to four pair of dress pants. I recommend khaki, gray, black, charcoal, or navy. If you love dresses and skirts, have one to two of each that will coordinate with your blazers. Don't forget to add dark denim jeans. In many workplaces, dark denim is acceptable, as are khaki pants and other slacks. Keep in mind, the darker the denim, the more perceived authority you will have.
- **Managers—Shirts and Sweaters.** I recommend three to four blouses (a couple in a solid color and a couple with patterns), two to three sweater sets or cardigan-style sweaters you can wear with the blouses, a few shirts for layering under blazers and sweaters, and perhaps two nice T-shirts (not concert T-shirts or ones you'd wear gardening) that can be dressed up on casual Fridays.
- **Support Staff—The Accessories.** Have some fun here, just be mindful to try to keep within your capsule. Shoes (comfort and style are at the forefront here) can be flats, heels, boots, or booties. Necklaces, earrings, rings, scarves, pashminas. I also love a sharp computer bag. Style yourself from tip to toe—even for your technology!

The Finishing Touches

Now that you have the structure of what should be in your professional wardrobe, let's talk about an often-overlooked area that becomes a fashion faux pas—not paying attention to what I call the "finishing touches."

Making a great first impression encompasses more than having specific garments such as blazers, smart-looking slacks, and coordinating accessories. Our clothing goes beyond the first impression. It creates a lasting impression on your audience. It is a key aspect of your Personal Brand.

Whether you are shopping in person or online, ask yourself: "What would Lisa think?" Would I say keep it or return it to the rack? Use what I call **Lisa's 3 F's** to help guide you as to whether you give the salesclerk your credit card—or, if you've bought it online, print out a return label:

1. **Fit**—Does the item fit you? Can you button the blouse or shirt? Are there gaps or bulging buttons exposing too much skin? Does your pant hemline drag on the floor? I once had an admin who didn't believe in tailoring! All her pants dragged on the floor so everyone could see worn frays straggling behind her. Other areas to focus on are sleeve length, shirt length, and skirt length. If you must shift, tug at, or try to stretch it out to make it fit, face it, it doesn't! Put it back on the rack or get your money back.

   A word of encouragement: Don't get too hung up on size. All garments are made differently, and many commercial garments are mass produced for smaller frames. So those of us who are not built with said smaller frame must go up in size. Also consider investing in a great tailor.

2. **Flatter**—You've established that you can button or zip the item. Great! Now I want you to stand in front of the mirror. Is the item made for your body shape and personality? Where is your eye drawn? Does it flatter your body or are you staring at yourself and thinking, "Ugh, I

don't feel good in this?" It may be because the item isn't flattering on you.

When considering if an item is flattering, look at its fabric, patterns, and structure. Just because the item looks good on the mannequin or model doesn't mean it's right for you and your body shape. Trust your instincts.

3. **Focus**—To take "flatter" one step further, ask yourself and others: Where does your eye focus? Does it go straight to a body part that you want to deemphasize? Men, are you showing too much chest hair? Ladies, are you showing too much cleavage? The standards of what we wear to the office are different than what we wear to dinner with friends.

A Word about Tailoring

Find a tailor, stat! It's that important! As I mentioned earlier, unless you are going to have all your clothing custom-made (love this!), most clothes you will shop for are designed with only a few body shapes and sizes in mind. That results in buying a pant you can button, but the length might be too long. No worries: just bring them to a tailor for a good hemming. The result will be a pair of pants that fit you and flatter your body shape. It's a win-win.

At the end of the day, we don't want our clothing to distract from our message. Credibility comes when people connect with our full message, including what we wear.

SUCCESS EXERCISE

Now Try This 3-Step Exercise:

1. **Step 1: Go to your closet.** Survey your current wardrobe. With the strategies I just taught you, can you put together one or two capsule wardrobes?

2. **Step 2: Try on each item.** Think about my 3 F's. Ask yourself, does the item still fit me? Does it flatter my current body shape? Where do my eyes focus? When was the last time I wore it? If you're having doubts or feel less than fabulous in that item, please donate it. There is someone else in the world that needs it. We want to create an "active wardrobe" filled with clothes you can just pull out and put on. You can save a couple of things that are inspiration items you plan to wear again one day. But not too many! I don't want you to feel bad about yourself. I want you to feel energized when you open your closet door.

3. **Step 3: After trying on the clothes and donating items that don't serve you anymore, what is missing?** Make a targeted list. I'm giving you permission to shop. To stay focused and hopefully keep your budget in check, ask yourself before you buy: Does this item match at least three other pieces in my capsule? Does it align with my Personal Brand? If not, move on to the next item.

Groom or Doom!

You've spent all this time fine-tuning your gorgeous professional wardrobe. Your pants are tailored to just the right length, your jacket sleeves hit just above your wrist perfectly. You even took the time to iron your pieces to give them that brand new, crisp look.

Yet your prospect looks at you and thinks, *Whoa, look at that bed head*! Or *He's taken his five o'clock shadow look way beyond midnight*!

I am not saying run to the barber or beauty salon every morning. But I do want you to spend a few additional minutes putting the finishing touches to your appearance. This includes hair, face, hands, and body.

Men—Your Shorr-to-Shine grooming kit should include (at minimum): A great razor, hair gel for unruly hair, beard trimmers, nail clippers and a nail file, a moisturizer (there are many made for men), deodorant, and lip balm. Don't forget hand sanitizer and breath mints.

Women—Your Shorr-to-Shine beauty kit includes these essentials: A great razor, hair products that align with your hair type, hair spray, lotion for hands and feet, nail and toe clippers, a great nail file, deodorant, skin care products (from makeup remover to moisturizer), a great mascara, blush, and lipstick. If you don't wear a lot of makeup, those items are a perfect starting point. For those of us who love to wear more, include a neutral eyeshadow palette, eyeliners, and concealers. Include hand sanitizer and breath mints too.

Appearing Confident With Power Postures

I read a mind-blowing statistic in an infographic on Entrepreneur.com that said the brain processes visual images 60,000 times faster than it does text. That's less than a second to process visuals. That barely gives us time to breathe.

I was taught that it takes no more than seven seconds to make a great first impression. This new data blows my original teachings out of the water.

These stats came from pre-pandemic research. Now that we are primarily post-pandemic and have even lower attention spans due to our dependence on online tools like Microsoft Teams and Zoom, we must work even harder to hold our audience's attention.

Our clothing plays a co-starring role in this show! The other co-star is your nonverbal behavior. It's unsettling how quickly your audience can lose interest in you and your message merely from a perceived eye roll, crossing your arms, or a habitual glance at your smart phone every few minutes.

There are several types of nonverbal communication also commonly referred to as your body language:

- Facial expressions
- Posture—standing and sitting
- Appearance
- Eye contact
- Body position
- Physical space between you and your audience
- Physical touch

Think about your nonverbal communication this way: "We listen with our eyes." So what are others saying about you? As a leader seeking to build your credibility, it's imperative to intentionally consider each body movement and gesture when you're preparing to have a persuasive conversation with a member of your team, negotiate a new contract with a client, or conduct an interview or a virtual meeting. Each nuance we display is watched and judged; it's just human nature. A great rule of thumb is to prepare for each meeting with an end goal in mind, then focus on the elements that will get you there. Your appearance and nonverbal behavior must factor into that.

I booked a meeting with a key vendor, Julie, to review our current contract. In the past, Julie would have flown to my office. However, thanks to Covid, we met virtually. As soon as the video turned on, I noticed she was sitting at her kitchen table. A clean, organized countertop was her backdrop. I could see a black Keurig coffee maker with a small coffee cup sitting on a matching saucer next to it, some sort of blender, and a small green leafy plant. "I like her organization," I thought. Julie's appearance on camera was like her orderly kitchen. She was wearing a lovely cream-colored sweater, dainty pearl necklace, and a touch of makeup.

We started to discuss our year-in-review. Mid-conversation, Julie's eyes went wide, and her body shifted toward the countertop behind her. Her cat jumped onto the counter and was about to knock over the coffee cup! Without a word, she jumped out of the chair, grabbed her cat, and placed it swiftly onto the floor. It was my turn for my eyes to widen as I noticed Julie was wearing plaid pajama pants! Did I laugh or feel angry that she didn't fully prepare for our meeting? I'm happy she salvaged her coffee from burning her cat; however, I now had a less professional perception of Julie. She couldn't bother to get fully dressed for our meeting. What does that say about the standards of her company? We are all in the business of influence. And our nonverbal communication can either make or break a deal.

SUCCESS EXERCISE

Whether I am face-to-face with someone or online, I demonstrate this component as a game of charades. This is the best way to teach this concept. It also makes for a fun team-building and educational exercise to do during a staff meeting.

Here is a list of several postures. The left-hand column features Power Postures. These convey confidence and authority. The right-hand column shows postures and gestures that are Credibility Crushers. These diminish your authority by making you appear nervous and insecure.

Assign one of the postures or gestures to a team member. Ask him or her to act out the gesture. Have your other team members guess what they're doing. Once you reveal the posture, discuss the positive and negative consequences of each. Will the posture build credibility or crush it? Why?

Power Postures	Credibility Crushers
Stand tall, hands on hips and smiling—also known as the Wonder Woman or Superman pose	Standing and hunching your shoulders
Stand tall, one hand on hip	Shrugging your shoulders, as if to say, "I don't know"
Outstretched hand for a handshake with eye contact and a smile	Standing in front of a person but looking away from them while speaking
Sitting at a table, looking attentive and smiling at the speaker	Sitting at a table and looking down at your smart phone
Sitting at a table, slightly leaning in to show interest in the other person speaking	Sitting at a table leaning back with both hands behind head, as if to relax

Power Postures	Credibility Crushers
Virtual: sitting up, your camera is on, and you're smiling	Virtual: Looking sideways
Virtual: Show a thumbs up and smile when you agree	Virtual: You turn your camera off while others are speaking

Networking Like a Pro

With a shaking finger, Michael pressed the "join meeting" button on his Zoom invitation. He was thankful this was a virtual meeting because he was sure his client would see his heart pounding outside of his chest.

While inhaling and exhaling to try to maintain a professional composure, he practiced Zoom's "share screen" feature. Michael's quick eyes perused the pages, stopping at the page that reflected the current price next to his new, increased contract price. He rehearsed his speech for what seemed like the thousandth time, "We so value you as a client. We've never wavered in our service to you. We never raised your contract rates, especially through Covid. But now we need to raise prices . . ." His voice trailed off in fear and he muttered, "What if they say no? What if they want to find a new provider for their technology services?" He shifted his internal struggle to more hopeful thoughts. "We've been giving them great service; we have a great relationship with them. What am I worried about?"

This was his first time meeting with this client to discuss their contract, which hadn't been reviewed over the six years since Michael's colleague Noah brought them on as a new client. This was a necessary discussion.

Suddenly, the window popped up, snapping Michael out of his internal conversation. He clicked the "admit now" button. His client turned on their camera and greeted Michael with a smiling "Hello!"

Michael smiled back and started to make small talk. "Hey John! How are the kids?" he asked with a jovial tone.

John proudly shared that his oldest was almost done with freshman year of college.

After a few minutes of friendly banter, Michael sat up in his seat and cleared his throat. With an even and empathetic tone of voice, Michael began his rehearsed speech. "We so value you as a client. I can't believe six years have gone by." Silently cheering himself on, he mustered the confidence to continue. "We have been so proud of the relationship we've built together. I know your company is more productive and secure since we took over as your IT provider. Noah and I have not raised your prices, especially through Covid, however I'd like to have that discussion with you now."

John widened his eyes, raised his brow slightly, and lightly shook his head in agreement. "I knew this conversation was coming. So, what do you have in mind?"

Michael gave a close-mouthed smile and nodded back in relief and acknowledgment. "Let me share my screen so we can review the price increases together."

Michael was ready. He'd done his research. He'd reviewed the hours spent working with this client, the price increases he was receiving from his vendors, and the margin he needed to make.

The contract, while significantly higher in price, was priced fairly. After more than 30 minutes of calm discussion, analysis, and a bit of negotiation, Michael and John agreed to renew the contract at Michael's newly proposed price. It was a 100% increase!

Peering down at the agenda Michael created for the meeting, he scrolled down at the last item that said, "Ask for Referral." Feeling a great sense of gratitude toward John, Michael said, "I have one more question."

John jokingly retorted, "I hope it is not to buy anything else right now!"

Michael chuckled, "No, I promise! I so value you as a client and would love more like you. If you have any colleagues who need our help, please let me know."

With a quick upturn of his head and eyes gazing toward the ceiling, John said, "I'd love to refer you. I have a few colleagues in mind. Let me reach out to them and let you know."

Michael thanked John. After a few more minutes of wrap-up and setting next steps, Michael and John each hit the "end meeting" button.

With great satisfaction, Michael slapped his hands on his desk and let out an exuberant *YES!*

Feeling more at ease, he thought about why this call was a success. Why had he been so worried? He'd always had a great relationship with John. His company was responsive to John's needs and his service team worked hard to give John legendary service too.

Michael reveled in his success for a few more minutes before inhaling a deep breath once again. Checking his calendar, Michael's excitement turned back to focus. *Sonya is not as easy-going as John and I need to raise her prices too,* he thought. Feeling slightly more empowered and confident in what he would say, he began contemplating how Sonya would react and began the rehearsal process all over again.

What Does Networking Have to Do With Building Your Personal Brand?

The "N" in my B.R.A.N.D. Method is all about networking—getting out there and cultivating relationships. I like to say that the other four letters of the B.R.A.N.D. Method are the physical and cognitive side of building your Personal Brand. The letter N is all about putting the others into action. We prepare our mindset, our values, our appearance, and our posture. We learn about our target audience and what keeps them up at night. We prepare our services and solutions to solve those unique needs.

Now it's time to **get out and network!** Go ahead and unleash your brand! Connecting with others on a human level, displaying empathy and integrity, is where your Personal Brand will really grow and build loyal, long-lasting relationships.

There are three key types of networking. No single one is more important than any other. To build your business, you need to take stock of each. They are:

1. **Client Business Review Meetings**—Networking with your clients to demonstrate relevance and strength;

2. **Lead Generation Networking**—Attending association meetings and events to generate new leads;

3. **Service Team Networking With Clients**—Opening up your mindset to the amazing opportunity your service

team has to build trusting relationships with your clients on a day-to-day basis.

Let's explore how to apply each of these into your business right away.

Client Business Review Meetings

One of the biggest lessons I learned while building my technology business was the importance of meeting regularly with our clients. Once you sign a new client, it is your responsibility to consistently demonstrate that your business is strong and relevant to their needs.

I've had to do a lot of damage control and missed out on big sales opportunities because my business was too busy running on a reactive hamster wheel rather than proactively seeking ways to enhance client relationships.

If you are not meeting with your clients at least on a quarterly basis, ask yourself—why not? What excuses are you telling yourself? Here are some of the many benefits to meeting with your clients.

1. **Demonstrate that you are still a viable and strong business**—If they don't hear from you, they may think you are either withering away or have gotten too big to handle the needs of their small business.

2. **Feedback on your business**—Ask your client: "How are we doing?" This powerful question shows your vulnerability and that you value this mutual relationship. It also provides valuable insights and training opportunities to make your team even stronger.

3. **Feedback on their company**—Instead of allowing concerns to fester and balloon, these meetings can also serve as an opportunity to say to your client, "I am concerned about ______." Maybe the client is unaware of an existing issue or doesn't really understand it and will use this meeting to gain clarity. You will also learn about potential expansion, staffing changes, new projects on the horizon and so much more.

4. **Sales opportunities**—Though you don't want every client meeting to be focused around presenting a new quote, there are lots of profits to be had here. You want to earn the sale before your competitor does. See how profitable these meetings are by tracking your success. You will be amazed at the results and proud of yourself for making the concerted effort.

5. **Share good news and company updates**—Share any new awards, your growth, even family updates. This is a wonderful time for some bonding.

At a minimum, you want to meet with your clients at least once per quarter. Depending on the number of clients you have, this could be more frequent if time permits.

You might be thinking, *I don't have the time to prepare, or even know where to begin.* I understand; I've been in your shoes. I want my client Michael's success story to be your story. So let's break this process down. We'll assume you are going to meet with your clients quarterly. We'll call them **Quarterly Business Review** meetings, or QBRs.

PREPARATION AHEAD OF MEETING

Quarterly Business Review meetings, really any meetings, are most successful when you prepare ahead of time. Let's walk through the process Michael used to conduct his meeting with his client to get that amazing increase.

I am going to put a twist on the traditional acronym.

- **Q—Qualify** your top list of clients. Don't let time be an excuse. Instead, ask yourself: Who are my top clients that I want to nurture and grow? Who values the product or service I offer? To help answer this question, look at revenue, profitability, historic growth, and overall likability. How easy are they to work with?
- **B—Block Off Time** on your calendar. You've started the process, now keep going! You are more likely to follow through with this process if you make the commitment and block off time on your calendar.
- **R—Review** account history and determine upsell opportunities. First, look at the types of services you've provided since the last meeting—or maybe the past year. Was it smooth sailing or bumpy waters? Were any big projects completed? Next, determine opportunities for growth. Did you launch any new products or services? Are you looking for a contract renewal? Are any changes needed to their contract?

  It's meeting day! Impress your clients by being organized and prepared. Here is a proven 6-step process that has earned many small business owners and sales managers immense success.

SUCCESS TIP

Every meeting is meant to be a relationship-building opportunity. However, not every QBR is meant to be an *upsell* opportunity. Use your judgment.

- **Step 1—Have an agenda**—Be sure to have structure to your meeting. This will show attention to detail, keep you on track, and show respect for your clients' time.
- **Step 2—Ask for feedback**—Open the discussion with "How are things going?" or "I'd love to hear your thoughts on the service we've been providing." Ask open-ended questions. Listen with empathy, while putting your ego aside. Take great notes and thank them often for their feedback, as this is the information you need to be able to grow.
- **Step 3—Ask if there are any projects on the horizon**—Once you've received feedback and had opening conversations, now say, "Tell me, do you have any plans for expansion? Are you moving? Any changes to your company?" Be friendly and see what you uncover. These could be up-sell opportunities for future meetings.
- **Step 4—Review account history**—Do you have reports that demonstrate growth? Mention hours spent servicing this client. Show photographs of projects completed. Maybe you've designed a new website? You can review analytics and user experience. If, like Michael, you manage your client's

IT network, you can review all the work you've done and share how you've made their company data more secure.

- **Step 5—Present recommendations**—Notice that this is not the first step! You need to exercise some empathy first. Determine the emotional state of the client and whether this is the right time to present new quotes or contract renewals. Remember that you are doing your client a true and needed service by presenting new products and services. Companies evolve and grow. So too should the products and services you offer.

- **Step 6—Ask for referrals**—This is an important marketing opportunity, so don't skip this step. If you are not sure what to ask, try this: "I'd love more clients like you! Can you refer me to your clients and colleagues who will also benefit from my services?" Often, clients will reply with "You bet! Let me give it some thought, and I'll see what I can do."

One last suggestion. Before you officially end the meeting, try to schedule your next meeting. This will help set future intentions and develop meeting consistency.

Get Out and Network—Generate Those Leads!

Networking to generate leads is not easy, especially if you're an introvert. Not to mention, you wear many hats that fill your day. However, getting out and networking is critical to the growth of both your Personal and Corporate Brands.

Before you turn the page and skip this critical section, let me convince you otherwise. Start with the many benefits of networking. This list is not in order of importance—because they're all important:

1. Letting your peers and prospects know that **you exist.**

2. Making **new relationships** or joint venture partnerships with complementary businesses. Don't let this opportunity pass you by.

3. Letting your clients know you are **still in business**.

4. Opportunity to **introduce new products** and services.

5. **Generate new LEADS**. You might be saying, "I don't need this, Lisa, I build my business on client referrals." That's great. However, to exponentially grow your business, you need more than referrals.

6. Become known as the **celebrity expert** in your industry. This is my favorite reason. I truly believe in focusing on one or two verticals to grow your business. Notice that this book was written for "small business owners." All its efforts, language, stories, and teachings focus on helping you grow. I want you to see that I empathize with what keeps you up at night and demonstrate how I am building credibility with you.

OK, let's explore the multitude of ways to network. This list is focused on lead generation and developing joint venture partnerships.

- **Attend Specialized Industry Associations**—You can't be an expert everywhere, so decide where it will be most profitable for you and where you can become a Brand Building Rockstar! For example, if you specialize in servicing lawyers, think about attending, presenting at, or sponsoring Bar Association events. If small medical practices are your focus, make your presence known at the Medical Associations where your clients and prospects are.

- **Host Webinars**—It's a great way to showcase your expertise and educate your clients and prospects. **Success Tip**: To maximize exposure, record your webinars. You can then post them to your social channels and make mini training videos based on various topics you've discussed.
- **Online Classes With Breakout Sessions**—Take advantage of breakout sessions to get to know other participants.
- **Attend Virtual Events**—Networking is not just in-person anymore. Be open to new ways to make new friends. For more details on virtual networking, see page 100 for "Don't Lose Connection While Virtual Networking."
- **Attend Chambers of Commerce Events**—This is a great place to meet a variety of business owners to help spread your message.
- **Meet 1:1 With Joint Venture (JV) Partners**—Book coffee meetings or virtual Zoom meetings to share ways you can work together or refer business to each other.
- **Network With Clients**—See QBR discussion above.
- **Network With Your Vendors**—Vendors can be a great referral source. Many often have what's called marketing development funds, or MDF. These are funds given to their

clients to help them supplement the cost of a marketing activity or event in an effort to expand their existing business. Ask your vendors about MDF. You'll be surprised how much money is available.

- **Conferences**—Attend conferences in your own industry. You never know whom you'll meet.
- **Technical, Trade Schools, or Any Relevant Educational Institution**—This is a great source for potential JV partners, possible leads, and even interns for your company. We all could use more help.
- **Anywhere**—You never know when an opportunity will arise. I once brought on a new client after meeting her at the grocery store. Take a moment to think: Where is the most unexpected place you found a new client?

From Tongue-tied to Confident—Use These Conversation Starters

I'm often asked, "Lisa, I always feel so awkward at networking events. I never know what to say. Can you help me?"

Yes! I agree. Networking is not the easiest marketing strategy, however, nothing in the world is more impactful than face-to-face human interaction.

The key is to *get others to talk*. To develop a meaningful relationship, you've got to demonstrate empathy during your conversation. This is also perfect if you are more introverted and not too comfortable sharing. Get your colleague to share. Most people love to talk about themselves. Don't be "that" person who is perceived as self-centered. We all dread encountering them at an event. Instead, ask many open-ended questions using an interested tone of voice.

Here Are 10 Quick Shorr-to-Shine Conversation Starters:

1. How are you involved in this organization?
2. Whom do you know here?
3. Tell me about your favorite book.
4. What are some of your hobbies?
5. Why did you get involved in this organization?
6. Tell me about your career journey.
7. Tell me more about what you do as an Operations Manager, Sales Manager, _________ (add in other roles).
8. Tell me about the products and services you offer.
9. What's been your favorite vacation destination? Why?
10. What is the biggest problem you solve for your clients?

Use these questions during virtual networking events too.

Be intentional with your questions. Take care *not* to ask yes or no questions—such as:

- Are you here for work?
- Do you like this venue?
- I like the appetizers here, do you?
- How long have you been at your company? (Even though this is not a yes/no answer, it will stop your conversation dead in its tracks!)

What if you need to bow out of a conversation? Either you've gathered the information you need or deemed this person not the best fit to continue networking with. You want to walk away from a discussion while maintaining credibility.

If this is someone you *are* interested in pursuing, I suggest you say something like: "I really enjoyed our talk. I am on a mission to meet three other people tonight. Can we schedule a coffee meeting to continue our conversation?"

If it's someone you *are not* interested in, say: "I really enjoyed our talk. I see another colleague I'd like to catch up with. Good luck with everything."

While you are practicing what to say during networking events, here are a few more etiquette tips to ensure you are Shorr-to-Shine!

1. **Place your name tag on your right lapel**. This is meant to align with your right-handed handshake. Your body naturally turns to the right when you extend your hand, allowing your eye to easily glance at your name tag.

2. **Dress for success**. Dress for the event you are attending and how you want to be perceived by others. (Refer to your "Fashion Goals" mentioned in Chapter 6.)

3. **Don't stuff your face with appetizers**. Sounds obvious, but I've been the recipient of one too many crumbs from other peoples' speaking and spewing! Not a great memory. Also, be mindful of your alcohol intake. Remember, netWORK means you are working while attending events. You always need to put your best foot forward.

4. **Give a firm handshake, along with eye contact and a smile**. Offer a confident first impression. If you're uncomfortable shaking hands, a fist-bump with eye-contact and a smile will do just fine these days.

5. **Fresh breath**. Yes, bring breath mints. Heavy perfume and cologne—no. You want to be remembered for your value, not the possibly unpleasant scents wafting from your body.

6. **Nonverbal behavior matters**. Do you look approachable because you're smiling? Or do you have a scowl on your face? How are you standing? Are you directly facing the person you are speaking to, or do you look like you see a delicious tray of scallops wrapped in bacon and are tempted to make a run for them before the other scavengers—I mean attendees—devour them?

7. **Show interest in your words and tone**. Show interest in your voice and curiosity in your tone. Say, "Really?" "Tell

me more." "You taught me something new!" This is not the time to air grievances or gossip about the colleague standing near you. Keep the conversation light and friendly.

8. **Stay away from conversations about politics, religion, race, gender**. Shift the conversation to the weather, their career journey, hobbies, why they are at this event.

9. **Bring business cards or some way to be able to follow-up with a hot prospect.** Too many people forget this step and miss a great opportunity.

Follow up! If you say you are going to, be sure you do. Show your prospect you are attentive and excited to grow a relationship with them.

Don't Lose Connection While Virtual Networking

The year 2020 was one the entire globe will never forget. The pandemic turned a world craving and thriving on human interaction into a world of extreme separation. Panic blanketed our globe like a howling blizzard. We all needed to scramble to figure out how we were going to remain connected to our families, friends, employees, and clients.

The day the announcement was made to "stay home," I slowly looked away from the evening news and toward my husband, as a pang of panic pounded my brain. With trepidation in my voice, I said, "What do we need to do to show empathy to our team and clients and keep our business going?" Eric's desperate eyes met mine. With equal uncertainty in his voice he responded, "We need to figure it out."

As technology providers, we knew "the cloud," or products and services accessed via the internet, would need to take center stage. Through all the trauma of the pandemic, cloud-based technology rose to the occasion to offer a new way to stay connected. Thankfully, for some businesses, the notion of a remote or hybrid workforce was already emerging, and we started to see coworking spaces and online platforms grow in popularity.

The first item Eric and I changed was our mindset. Since 1992, Secure Future Tech Solutions had always had employees work together on-site. Never did we envision the ability to survive, let alone thrive, if we all worked from home.

We embraced online tools, including Microsoft Teams and Zoom. We established a daily morning team meeting to check in and see how each person was feeling and what technical help they needed to help support our clients.

Each client's scope of work suddenly expanded to include setting up "new" home offices in bedrooms, kitchens, living rooms—wherever they could gain internet access.

Web cameras flew off the shelves, as did toilet paper and cleaning supplies. I recall donating my office desk webcam to a distressed client who had a vital meeting to conduct.

The early stages of our online team meetings looked like a harried version of the TV show *Hollywood Squares*. Bedhead, zombie attire, chaotic backgrounds, grainy cameras, lighting from a horror movie—the list could go on!

Everyone was so focused on connecting that we developed a tolerance for these less-than-ideal images.

Now that you are reading this book, I am here to affirm, enough is enough! Virtual networking and connecting is here to stay. As a leader, you need to either rebuild or maintain your strong influencing skills when in a remote setting. There are nuances to virtual networking that make this more challenging than in-person. This is such an essential tool when building your brand and business. You've got to take note.

So how do you go from harried *Hollywood Squares* to the polished "squares" of *The Brady Bunch*? Use this checklist as your guide:

- **Mindset**—A colleague once told me that virtual networking is like having several 1:1 meetings. You must impress and connect with each one. This is an important mindset to have when pressing the "join meeting" button.
- **Camera placement**—No more cut-off faces or looking into the tunnels of your nostrils! I also want to see your entire face and not just your lovely profile. As mentioned, your eyes and smile are even more important virtually since that is essentially all we see from our computer screen. Place your camera directly in front of your face. If you want to appear as if you are looking directly at your audience, look at the "light" and lens on the actual camera and not at the person you are talking to.
- **Illuminate your face**—Now that you've set up your camera properly, let's focus on proper lighting and placement. There are many lighting options on the market today. Google the terms *video* or *podcast lighting* and a plethora of options will show up. The key is to place your lighting in front of your face. Many professional studios have two lighting stands placed diagonally on either side of a face, so the light is not directly in the eyes. Be sure to reduce any light behind you, or you'll look like you've been sucked into a thick hazy cloud.

- **Amp up your voice with an external microphone**—Don't leave your message to chance with a built-in microphone, especially if you have an old computer. Don't frustrate your client or prospect because they missed your message or critical response to their issue. Instead, invest in an external microphone that makes you sound like you are hosting a podcast or ready to deliver a keynote address. We want your message to be heard loud and clear.

- **Speak slower and louder**—Not everyone will have the best tech, nor will their virtual offices be in the quietest of spaces. To really be engaging during a virtual networking event or online meeting, speak a bit slower than usual, taking care to enunciate your words. You'll also want to speak a bit louder to accommodate those audience members who don't have great speakers.

- **Say their name**—To SHOW you are paying attention and really build rapport, initiate conversations by saying others' names. Our connection to our name is primal. It's one of the first words we learn to identify ourselves. Say statements such as, *"Jim—tell me about your company."* Or *"I agree with you Chantel, your new office wall color is such a calming shade of blue!"*

- **Nonverbal behavior matters**—Let me get it out there: "WE SEE YOU!" We see you looking at your phone. We see you talking to your dog. We see you looking away. We see you slouching. We see you sneering. We see you rolling your eyes. We see you getting up. We see you in a side conversation, looking like you're in a silent Charlie Chaplin movie. Does any of that behavior show you respecting your audience or demonstrating any leadership qualities? Let your audience see you smiling, positively nodding your head, looking forward, and sitting up properly in your chair positioned in the center of your screen. That sets the right engaged message.

- **The battleground background**—You can infer quite a bit about a person by looking at their background. Your eyes might fixate on mountainous stacks of manila folders bursting with dog-eared papers and think, "Geez, if that's a mess, will their work be a mess too?" Not only were you distracted by the conversation, but you also made a *potentially* incorrect interpretation about your colleague's quality of work. It's best to stage your background to appear neat and tidy. There are also a variety of virtual backgrounds you can select from. If you choose this route, just be sure you are in the center of the camera so that your arm or head don't disappear as if you're getting "beamed up" by Scotty in *Star Trek*.
- **Turn On Your Camera**—I saved the best for last: Turn on your camera! Unless you absolutely must have a side conversation, run to the bathroom, or take a bite of your sandwich, please leave your camera on. Having your camera off displays a lack of preparedness, disinterest in the conversation, and overall disrespect for the meeting host and guests.

As the leader of your company, you set the tone for all behavior within your organization. Show up and be present by having your camera on, appear professional, speak confidently, and engage your audience.

How Your Team Sells Without Actually Selling

Think of a client you know who needs your products or services but just won't make the move. Every time they see you or your sales rep coming, they make a quick beeline in the other direction, as if you're the money monster looking to steal all their cash.

When you finally get a meeting booked, you hear in an accusatory tone, "What are you trying to sell me now?"

Imagine me giving you a great big empathetic hug! Sales is so hard, but the results are so rewarding.

You need all the sales reinforcements you can get to influence your clients to see the light and convince them that they need your products and services.

Have you ever considered your staff to be salespeople? Think about it. They are working with your clients on a daily basis. They are viewed as their clients' problem solvers or "trusted advisors"—not someone who just wants to sell them something (even though you and I know the client may need it).

I'm not saying they must be deal-closers. Rather, if they have a wonderful rapport with your clients, they are the perfect person to cultivate the sales process by "planting seeds."

Consider this example from my technology business. My client George, owner of a growing plumbing supplies company, did not like to spend money on technology. He consistently avoided phone calls and booking meetings with our sales team. With a shrug of his shoulders and a confident tone, George would always reply, "Eh, we're fine. Nothing bad has happened so far."

One of George's biggest culprits was a very old Windows Server 2008. This 12-year-old server was no longer supported by Microsoft, which meant no security upgrades and no way to utilize Microsoft's expertise should my technical team need it. The biggest risk, which my sales team tried repeatedly to convey, was a shutdown of the entire network, which would render the company unable to work.

Our president, Eric, decided to take a different approach. Although George was too busy to meet with him, Eric decided to have George's favorite engineer, Kurt, have a chat with him instead.

It was 9:00 a.m. and time for our daily virtual all-staff meeting. Once the team logged in, Eric drew everyone's attention by saying a friendly "Good morning, everyone! It's Tech-Tip Tuesday, and I'd like our conversation to be around one of our clients. Let's talk about George's server." Eric quickly shifted his tone from upbeat to urgent. "I've tried repeatedly to tell him about the dire risks, but he won't take my call. Kurt, when are you scheduled to visit their office?"

Hearing his name, Kurt, perked up and took himself off mute. "I'm going back tomorrow. I agree. That server needs to go."

"Glad we're on the same page," Eric said with relief. "When you're there, please talk to George about the server. Maybe if he sees *you*, he won't feel like you're just trying to sell him something. I know he really likes and trusts you, Kurt."

"What do you want me to say?" A look of panic crossed Kurt's face. "I'm not a salesperson."

"Exactly," Eric replied. "I'd like you to say with concern in your tone, 'George, I'm worried about your server. It's 12 years old and no longer supported by Microsoft. You are extremely vulnerable to a cyber-attack and a complete shutdown of your business. Can I have Eric call you to discuss replacing it?"

After a bit of role-playing and further discussion, Kurt felt better about the approach and gladly agreed to make the recommendation.

Kurt arrived on-site and had his discussion with George as practiced. To Kurt and Eric's surprise, George actually said, "No need to have Eric call me. Just have him send me the quote and I'll sign it."

Kurt immediately let Eric know to send the quote right away. Within a few days, a new server was quoted, signed, and on order! Bam! A project value of $20,000—and one that would solve a huge issue.

This is one of many stories I share with my service team, who have great rapport with our clients and have made recommendations to support the sales process.

I am making the case that your entire team is networking with your clients and prospects every day, not just those directly involved in business development. It's crucial to ensure your entire team has a polished Personal Brand and the ability to establish great connections to provide not just good customer service, but a great client experience.

Here Are 7 Impactful Tips to Establish Rapport to Become That Trusted Advisor:

1. **Professional Appearance**—Clients love consistency. Show up every time with a smile and wearing your corporate uniform (or at least not appearing to have just rolled out of bed and grabbed the cleanest of your dirty T-shirts out of the hamper). Remember—grooming!

2. **Understand the Client's Emotional State**—Exercise Emotional Intelligence to manage your emotions and do all you can to ensure your client remains calm and reassured.

3. **Don't Assume the Client Understands or Even KNOWS Their Issue**—Remember, they hired you to be the expert in an area in which they are not. Be mindful that just because you understand an issue, your client also understands it. They probably don't. Ask a lot of questions to get to the root of the problem.

4. **Use ACTIVE L.I.S.T.E.N.ing Skills to Demonstrate Understanding and Validate Clients' Needs**. Mistrust sets in when your client doesn't feel heard or understood. So ask questions and reply with confidence.

5. **Clear, Calm, and Respectful Tone of Voice**—As I mentioned earlier, I love this saying by the late Maya Angelou: *"I've learned that people will forget what you said, people will forget what you did, but people will never forget how you made them feel."* There are many interpretations of this saying. One lies in the importance of using a respectful, empathetic tone of voice. Your tone is the vocal way to show you understand and are there to help. An angry or disinterested tone, even using the same words, could be interpreted quite differently.

6. **No Geek Speak! No Acronyms! Speak Their Language**—Talk to your team about ways to turn your industry lingo and terminology into digestible and understandable terminology for your clients. Show your clients you are "all in" and invested in their business growth. A great strategy is to use metaphors or analogies to help explain complicated scenarios.

7. **Make Small Talk**—Focus on sports, weather, pets, travel plans, and family celebrations. It is poor etiquette to talk about religion or politics or get involved in your clients' office gossip.

You've got rapport established. Check!

Now, let's break down my **S.E.E.D. Process** that enables your team to become the ultimate referral machine!

S See the issue or opportunity

E Engage the client in discussion

E Engage the sales department once a recommendation is made

D Deploy the results!

S—See the Issue—Train your team to be on the lookout for opportunities or impending issues. Explain that they're your eyes and ears at your client's site more frequently than you are. This also makes for important and productive staff meeting discussions. Remember—your support staff is not meant to be told or believe they are sales closers, merely conversation starters. If they see something, train them to say something.

E—Engage the Client in the Discussion—Once a need has been identified, coach your team members on what to say, how to make a recommendation, and how to plant a seed. Show pride and respect for your team members and the wonderful relationship they have with your clients. This will help boost their confidence in making suggestions to clients. To make this process even smoother, I have three conversation starters for you below.

E—Engage the Sales Department—Your team member has made a recommendation, and the client says, "Sure, I'll talk to sales." Now that team member must be trained to bring this hot lead back to you so your sales team can follow up right away. Your action needs to be swift—strike while the iron is hot!

D—Deploy the Results—A satisfying reward is your team writing, deploying, installing, painting, creating, or rewiring whatever was sold.

A caveat: Not every seed that is planted will result in a sale. But many will, or at least open the door to further discussion. I'd love to hear your success stories! Send them to me at lisa@shorrsuccess.com.

WHAT SHOULD YOU SAY? HERE ARE THREE CONVERSATION STARTERS.

These are the exact phrases I use when I'm coaching my tech team or my clients' teams. They are universal and meant to be delivered in an urgent, yet empathetic tone. Your job is to fill in the blanks with the products and services you offer that will improve your clients' current business state.

1. **Have you thought about . . .**
   . . . upgrading your computer? . . . it will run faster, be compatible with your software, be more secure . . .

2. **I'm concerned about . . .**
   . . . your server crashing . . .
   . . . the security on your network . . .

3. **Hey, I noticed . . .**
   . . . your phones sound choppy . . .
   . . . when I was installing your . . .

Once the recommendation has been made, close with:

"I'll have Lisa (replace my name with the correct person in your Sales Department) reach out to you to discuss."

SUCCESS EXERCISE

Now you try!

Brainstorm a variety of areas that could be recommended to your clients. Think about ways to make your clients more secure, more productive, in compliance, more beautiful, more innovative, or stand out from their competition. Once your list is compiled, practice role-playing what to say to each client in each scenario. This will prepare each team member to be in the right mindset when the opportunity arises. It will also help polish their conversation.

CHAPTER 8

DYNAMIC DIALOGUE

It was 3:45 p.m. on a Monday afternoon. I was gingerly sipping a latte in a local café while making last minute updates to my notes.

At 4:00 p.m. sharp, the door to the coffee shop swung open. A young woman marched inside. She was wearing athletic attire—beige leggings and a maroon polo shirt. Her light brown hair fell below her shoulders, giving her a youthful appearance. I knew this was Katherine when I looked at her serious eyes. She looked like she was on a mission, and it was to have a discussion with me.

I was hired by Katherine's boss Christine, co-owner of a busy physical therapy practice, to help solve a problem: an abrasive manager (Katherine) whom no one wanted to work with.

Christine and I had met days earlier at this same coffee shop. Through an initial friendly conversation, we realized that although we'd lived in different cities when we were in high school, Christine and I had attended the same national dance school. We smiled at the revelation and bonded over ballet! Christine's bright smile faded when we began talking about Katherine. She'd received consistent complaints from Katherine's coworkers of abrasive behavior. "Essentially," Christine began in a perplexed tone, "I'm at my wits' end. I know Katherine is passionate and a good physical therapist, and our clients seem happy, but as a manager, she is making her team angry. I already had one girl ask to move to another location."

I listened to Christine's concerns for several more minutes. We determined a course of action. I was hired to work with Katherine on taking ownership of and building her leadership skills. As part of my preparation work, I was given permission to interview a few of Katherine's colleagues so I could build their feedback into my training.

Each employee I called painted a similar picture of Katherine: confident and knowledgeable about PT and great with the clients, yet edgy and abrupt with the staff. In their own words, each employee wanted to see a warmer tone that encompassed more empathy toward others' ideas.

I knew I had my work cut out for me. But I have faith in the ability for all to grow if they are open to it.

I smiled and waved to Katherine. "Hello, I'm Lisa! I hope you are Katherine, or I just waved to the wrong person!" I said in an upbeat tone, hoping to put Katherine at ease.

"It's me. Nice to meet you," Katherine replied, in a friendly yet reserved tone.

Pointing to the menu board, I asked, "Can I get you a cup of coffee? The lattes are delish here."

"No thank you. I'd just like a bottle of water," Katherine responded.

I bought her a water and sat back down at our table for two. I began by asking, "What are the key ingredients in maintaining a successful relationship?"

Katherine sat silent for a moment, tapping her finger on the lid of her water bottle. While staring at it, she replied, "I have two answers. For my team, I need to be on the pulse of what is happening, making sure they are consistently following the systems we have in place. When they are not, I must give them feedback on how to correct it. We all need to take ownership for our failures. For our patients, I want to demonstrate knowledge but also empathy to show we understand and are listening to their needs."

I realized her beliefs on management/leadership focused more on logic and a task-based approach versus the softer approach she took with her patients.

Before I was able to respond, Katherine perked up in her seat and shared what seemed like a revelation. "I suppose my behavior might seem intimidating to the team."

I gave her an appreciative smile. I agreed and talked about how powerful the combination of the words you say, along with your tone of voice, are to a great team culture. And you, as the branch manager, set the standard for success. It's great to have processes and procedures; however, if others don't feel supported and are afraid to approach you, morale will inevitably decrease.

This discussion led to several other constructive coaching conversations together around tone of voice, rephrasing constructive feedback, and the power of nonverbal messaging.

Days afterward, Christine reported seeing an energy shift in Katherine's office interactions—from pragmatic and brazen to empathetic, collaborative communication.

I've worked with many business owners, managers, and teams who, like Katherine, are unaware of the emotional impact they have on those around them. Too often, words are spoken without taking care to consider how those words and, more importantly, the tone and nonverbal expressions that go with it, will make another person feel.

I call this strategy in my B.R.A.N.D. Method *Dynamic Dialogue* because when building your credibility, you must be intentional with the words you choose and, even more importantly, the nonverbal way you deliver your message. I want you to become the "celebrity" in your particular industry. That means you need to first listen and then respond in a manner that aligns with your authentic value words (remember to ask yourself, "How do I want to be perceived by others?") and with the values of your clients or prospects. This chapter is going to teach you the key building blocks to success.

Albert Mehrabian on Emotional Impact

(It's Not What You Say—It's How You Say It That Matters)

Do you know the purpose of your voice? It's to emotionally persuade your audience to take action. Your audience could be employees, clients, friends, prospects, family, children, or whomever you are in conversation with. You could be communicating one-to-one or one-to-many as a workshop facilitator or keynote speaker.

Researcher and professor emeritus from UCLA, Dr. Albert Mehrabian, was interested in studying emotional communication. In 1967, he conducted two studies to determine what the most effective components are when someone is expressing how they are feeling about a situation or a person. Where did the listener or viewer, depending on the study, apply the most emphasis?

The first study focused on vocal quality and facial expressions. Respondents listened to the same word delivered using multiple variations including speed, tonality, and pauses or hesitation.

Along with the word, respondents also looked at an image of a corresponding facial expression. Could the respondents discern the correct emotion being displayed?

The other study analyzed the impact of tone of voice with the spoken word. Listening to a series of nine words delivered using a variety of tones, respondents were asked to determine the emotion conveyed.

Dr. Mehrabian combined the results of both studies to create the 7-38-55 Communication Rule. The studies revealed that respondents were affected in the following ways:

- 7% by the words said
- 38% by the vocal quality of the voice
- 55% by nonverbal facial expressions

I love how this research focuses solely on "emotional communication." Most, but not all, purchasing decisions are based on emotion. You have now cracked the code on how to positively influence others to take action.

This theory does not apply to a non-emotional statement like "The report shows a spike in sales in the second quarter." That statement is matter-of-fact.

But suppose someone said to you, *"I am confused and don't understand the report you delivered."* The study applies here because the speaker shared a feeling of confusion. Now, envision hearing and seeing your client deliver this statement. According to the study, you will pay close attention to your client's tone of voice and facial expression before formulating a response.

To build a strong relationship, you are expected to pick up on those nonverbal cues and provide an empathetic response such as, "I'm sorry. I am happy to take a closer look. Please tell me which parts are confusing to you." Incidentally, a non-empathetic response, which could easily be a deal breaker, would be you stating in an agitated tone, "The report is straightforward. What don't you understand?"

I cringe just thinking about this response! Do you also cringe?

Each person in your company has a direct impact on the success of your business. Another point to note is that their vocal response may vary from role to role or department to department.

6 Vocal Variations (and 1 Facial Expression)

While facial expressions appeared to be the primary component to impactful communication, vocal tone came in a strong second. You may be able to mask an angry face. It's very hard, however, to mask frustration or disinterest in your tone. The minute you make your clients or prospects feel "not OK" they are googling your competitor's phone number.

I believe your voice and how you deliver your message is the most powerful component to building a respected and trusted Personal Brand. People might look past an unkempt appearance, but they sure won't forget an agitated or disinterested tone.

To understand the power of our vocal quality even further, let's break down the foundations of our voice. Some public speakers call this voice modulation, essentially using variation in your voice.

Imagine you are preparing for a presentation at your local Chamber of Commerce. They asked you to speak about *"The 5 Lessons I Learned From Entrepreneurship."* This is your big moment to start building a name for yourself with this organization!

Excited, you spend hours putting together your presentation. You've prepared slides and charts. You even ironed your shirt and pants!

The day has arrived. With excitement, the MC announces your name. You take a deep breath and walk in front of the audience. The butterflies in your stomach seem to fly to your throat when you notice the sea of eyes focused on you. Sweat begins to bead on your forehead. To gain composure you take another deep breath, and a smile appears on your face. You begin to speak. Someone from the audience calls out, "Will you please speak louder?"

"Um, sure, sorry!" you mutter. You raise your volume, but now feel like you are screaming. A few minutes later, you notice the sea of eyes originally focused on you begin to look away. One person is staring at their smart phone, another leans over and speaks to another attendee. You try not to notice and keep going.

Finally, your presentation ends. You let out a sigh. What went wrong, you wonder? How did I lose their attention?

Has this ever happened to you?

When building your brand, public speaking is an important strategy to establish credibility. It's critical to sound authentic, confident, and interesting. The goal is to **inspire, influence, and persuade** your audience to **listen, learn, and act**.

Next time you are preparing for any presentation or meeting, incorporate these six vocal foundations and one facial expression.

1. Inflection

2. Speed

3. Volume

4. Tone

5. Pausing

6. Enunciation

7. Facial expressions

Let's take a deeper dive into each.

- **Inflection**—Think about your favorite song. Now, take a moment to sing it. Do you feel your voice go up and down in melody in alignment with the beat of the accompanying music? This concept is the same for public speaking. Too often, however, speakers get stuck in speaking in just one "melody"—monotone. Monotone can be one excited tone, or a bland, disinterested tone maintained throughout an entire presentation. Without variation, the audience has no idea what key points are most important for them to learn. When you add inflection, or emphasis on certain words or phrases, you give your audience clues as to where to take notice. Inflection adds energy and variation to your presentation.

- **Speed**—Your rate of speaking is important. It tells the listener your excitement for something or makes something sound so important that we slow down our speech. Suppose I said to you, *"I have something to tell you."* If I said it at a fast pace with a higher pitch, your perception could be: *Yikes! What in the world is wrong*?! What if I said that same comment at a slower rate with a jovial emphasis on the word "something": "I have *something* to tell you." Now your energy turns from anxious to excited to know what that something is.

- **Volume**—Too often, speakers and managers are caught in too soft a range because they are nervous or concerned about appearing too aggressive. Softness can be tricky when it comes to perception. It might be nice to be perceived as soft-spoken, but you might also be perceived as lacking confidence. Conversely, speak too loudly and you may be perceived as aggressive. Your volume will need to be modified each time you speak, depending on your audience.

- **Tone**—There are two extremes with tonality. You'll either sound breathy and airy like Marilyn Monroe or raspy and edgy like Harvey Fierstein. Harvey Fierstein happens to have abnormal vocal cords that make his voice deep and raspy, but most of us do not. Often, an edgy, raspy tone is misunderstood as frustration or arrogance, while someone with too airy a tone is often not taken as seriously as their deeper-speaking colleague. Example: What if you say in a high-pitched or airy tone, "The price of this new service is $100." Try saying it yourself. What might you hear? "Well, that's nice but doesn't sound like I have to have it." Now say it in a slightly deeper, more confident voice. Do you hear either more urgency or at least a heightened sense of importance? Your tone is one of the most important verbal cues that determines whether your listener has a positive or negative experience.

- **Pausing**—Though this does not necessarily have to do with the sound of your voice, there's something very powerful when you make a statement, then pause and give the audience time to process what you are saying. Here's an example. Say this statement out loud with a deeper tone, emphasis, and a pause after the word "are": "The #1 cybersecurity threat to small businesses today are . . . phishing emails." If you said the entire sentence at a fast pace with no inflection, the listener wouldn't have time to process and make sense of your words. By slowing down and pausing, you are adding interest and even intrigue to your statement.

- **Enunciation**—I was born just outside of Boston, Massachusetts, home of delicious seafood and notorious for natives dropping the "r" from our words. "Park the car," sounds like "Pahk the cah." For a short time, I moved across the country. In California, I felt that everyone properly pronounced every letter of the alphabet. Many of my new friends would either misunderstand what I was saying or make fun of my elocution. Elocution (the clarity with which we deliver our speech or our individual words), incorporates inflection, pauses, and tone, but also incorporates how clearly we pronounce each word. Example: Suppose you are in a restaurant and order toast, but they thought you said roast and bring you that instead? People from different regions of our nation/globe have different accents. If your accent differs from your audience's, you need to work a bit harder to enunciate each word so the message is heard and understood.
- **Facial Expressions**—Are you thinking, "Lisa, this one doesn't have to do with our voice, why add this here?" Because our facial expressions are powerful. Our emotions can include fear, disgust, surprise, happiness, sadness, and anger. When our face displays these emotions, typically our voice follows

SUCCESS TIP

Virtual Presence and Your Voice

It's even more difficult to connect with your audience in a virtual environment. All you have is what others see via their monitor. That monitor can be large or very small, like that on a cell phone. Take these size differences into account. Also consider that each person will have varying audio quality. Some will be tuning in with external speakers, others will use the audio built into their laptops, while others will have ear buds poked into their ears. Keep these key tips in mind:

1. Be mindful of your facial expressions on camera. This is all your audience sees. Be sure you appear to be paying attention and keep an interested smile on your face.

2. Speak a bit louder. Don't scream, just raise your volume so all can hear. A great external microphone should help clarify your audio. It's OK to ask your audience, "Can everyone hear me?"

3. Speak a bit slower. This will help your audience process what you are saying. Not so slow that you sound disinterested, just slow enough to help with enunciation and understanding.

4. Posture counts. Sit straight up and face forward toward your camera. If your camera is to the side of you, please move it in front of you so your audience can connect with you via your eyes and smiling face!

suit. In addition, hearing a tone and seeing that tone on your face reinforces the perception. So be careful to consider your facial expressions when you are in any meeting or conversation. You don't want your message to be misunderstood.

THE LEADER'S GUIDE TO COMMUNICATE TO BUILD TRUST

We've established that every person in your business is a leader in their respective roles and departments and impacts the success of your business. The way each person communicates is key in influencing relationships—both internally with coworkers and externally with clients and prospects.

The chart below highlights a speak "Like This" to inspire and build trust and "Not Like This" to lose trust.

Like This—Build Trust	Not Like This—Lose Trust
Show understanding and empathy in your tone	Sound monotone and disinterested
Use inflection and excitement in your voice to emphasize words of praise and communicate a job well done	Communicate only to correct behavior and use a frustrated tone when delivering feedback
Greet all team members with a cheery hello and a smile!	Barely say hello or look up from a computer screen, tablet, or smart phone
Answer phone with an interested and friendly greeting and smile in their voice	Answer phone speaking fast, soft, or in a monotone voice
Lead a meeting sounding confident, organized, and with purpose	Attend meetings sighing, rolling eyes, and speaking either too fast or slow as if distracted or as if this is a waste of time
Answer team questions with encouragement, showing confidence in that person's abilities	Bark answers when approached and make comments such as "I'll do it myself"

Like This—Build Trust	Not Like This—Lose Trust
When you don't know an answer you say, "I don't have an answer yet. Let me do some research and get back to you this afternoon."	"We can't do it." "It's not something we can do." "I don't know."
Set honest expectations regarding follow-up. Then follow up, even if the answer is not resolved right away.	Says, "I'll get back to you," then never follows up until client calls and asks. Leader then responds in an impatient tone, "I don't know yet. I said I'll get back to you."
Encourages team members to speak during a meeting by saying in a supportive tone, "Jamal, your feedback matters. I'd love to hear your thoughts on this project too."	Never offers the floor to the team; doesn't listen to others in the meeting; barks orders; makes others cower in fear

SUCCESS EXERCISE

Now you try. What would you add to my "Like This" "Not Like This" list? During a staff meeting, discuss the scenarios above. Ask, how does each make you feel? What are the consequences/impact to business growth? Finally, brainstorm other communication examples where a leader can use positive vocal ranges to foster collaboration and enhance team morale.

6 Steps to Maintain Credibility During Difficult Conversations

One of my managers poked her head into my office and asked in a concerned voice, "Lisa, can I talk to you a minute?"

"Sure, what's up?"

"Well, I'm not sure how to handle a situation I'm having with Jordan. A few team members have complained that Jordan has body odor. It's noticeable when they work with him on a client issue and walk by his cubicle. It's impacting the team, and I'm afraid a client might call us to complain. Can you please talk to him?"

I sat still a moment as panic permeated my body, landing in my now racing brain. So many fears ran through my mind. What did our clients think about Jordan and our company? If I don't handle this, will I lose team members? How will that impact morale? And most importantly, how can I help Jordan? He is such a wonderful employee and so talented. Does he even realize he has an issue?

When my mind finally came back to reality, I thanked my manager for bringing this to my attention and reassured her that I would speak to Jordan that afternoon.

My manager thanked me for "handling this difficult conversation" and left saying, "Let me know if I can do anything to help."

I sat for several minutes taking deep controlled breaths while pondering how I could best handle this situation. I thought back to a workshop where I taught business leaders the process I use when handling difficult situations. I logged back into my computer and double-clicked on the document I'd saved to my desktop for easy access.

As a business owner, you are faced with difficult conversations almost daily. This process helps maintain cool and credibility. My eyes stared at each strategy, while my mind silently considered each one.

1. Don't procrastinate.

2. Use Emotional Intelligence and diplomacy when assessing the situation.

3. Take deep breaths.

4. Watch your speed, tone, and volume.

5. 3 P's—Prepare, Practice, Present.

6. Use active L.I.S.T.E.N.ing skills.

I considered each strategy and formulated how I would handle the situation. I picked up the phone and dialed Jordan's extension.

"Hi, Lisa!" he said.

As friendly as could be, I replied, "Hey, Jordan, do you have a minute? I'd like to chat with you about something."

"No problem."

"Great. Can you come to my office?"

Within a minute, Jordan knocked on my door. I greeted him with a warm smile and said, "Come, have a seat."

Not wanting to incriminate any team members, I knew the best approach was to take ownership of the issue. I adjusted my body to make sure I was facing Jordan and said in a concerned tone, "I noticed a smell coming from your cubicle area and I'd like to talk about your body odor. How can I help you resolve this situation?" I paused to give Jordan time to process what I was asking and think about how he was going to respond.

Jordan shifted nervously in his seat. "I didn't realize I had a problem. I haven't been able to wash my company shirts often because I only have three."

"I totally get how hard it is to keep up with laundry. And I don't want this to end up impacting your relationships with the team. How about I provide you with a couple more company shirts, so you'll have one for each day of the week. Do you think that will help you wear clean shirts to the office?"

"Yes, I'd appreciate that." Jordan's brows dipped into a bit of a furrow, as he appeared a bit distressed about the situation. "I am sorry for this. I'll be more mindful. You won't have to speak to me about this again."

"Hey, no worries." He looked concerned; I looked back with an expression of empathy and reassurance. "Just keep in mind that good hygiene is important. If you need me to provide you with more shirts or need help with anything else, please let me know. You are such a valuable employee. I want to do all I can to support you. I'll have Len grab you a couple of additional shirts right away!"

Jordan stood up and thanked me once again. He opened my office door and swiftly walked back to his desk.

I took a deep breath and felt satisfied that I'd resolved this issue with patience and kindness. I was grateful that my trusty process helped me through yet another difficult conversation.

Difficult conversations include negotiations, handling difficult clients, firing employees, and private issues like the one I'd had with Jordan. Jumping into one of these discussions or any other difficult conversation (and there are so many!) unprepared will most likely cause you to react and respond in a way that either upsets the party you're in conflict with or hurts your credibility as a leader. How many times have you had a tough conversation and left it thinking, "Why did I say that?" or "I wish I had said that."

Difficult conversations are part of life. Earn more respect by being a leader known for choosing to deal with these situations tactfully and swiftly, head on.

To demonstrate how to incorporate this process, here is how I handled Jordan's situation.

1. **Don't Procrastinate**—Don't let difficult conversations fester. First, I needed to show my manager who privately came to me that I was listening and honoring her request. Second, I didn't want the situation with Jordan to get worse. I was concerned that my employees would become more upset and I would start receiving client complaint calls questioning our credibility and how we handle employee issues. This is not how I wanted my brand to be perceived.

2. **Use Emotional Intelligence and Diplomacy When Assessing the Situation**—I did not want to appear or sound insensitive when speaking with Jordan. I also did not want to alarm him by turning this into a defensive blame game. After assessing the scope and facts of the situation, I realized I needed to speak calmly—by slowing down my pace and softening my volume. I intentionally selected a non-accusatory, *I am taking ownership approach*, by starting with, "I noticed a smell . . ." I took care to modulate my voice to convey concern and genuine caring.

3. **Take Deep Breaths**—Taking measured deep breaths before, during, and after your meeting is paramount to calming your nervous system down. I sure needed this exercise when dealing with this unique issue.

4. **Watch Your Speed, Tone, and Volume**—Too often, difficult situations go south because we don't try to think

before we speak. Conversation is a two-way street. The way you deliver your message or response will likely elicit a similar response from the other party. I wanted Jordan to know this conversation was out of support and concern for his well-being. Not wanting to act too excited and unnerve Jordan, I took care to slow down my pace, add concern and compassion to my tone, and lower my volume so I sounded conversational versus heightened/upset. This helped to keep Jordan's nerves in check.

5. **3 P's—Prepare, Practice, Present**—My 3 P's is a great rule of thumb for any meeting or presentation you must deliver. Prepare what you are going to say or the response you plan to deliver. Practice saying and resaying the scenario to gain familiarity and comfort. By the time you present, you will have greater confidence and control over your delivery. In Jordan's case, I needed to gather my facts and think about the verbal and nonverbal language I wanted to use to broach this subject with him. Because I took time to gather my thoughts and emotions around this, I was able to have a productive and constructive conversation.

6. **Use Active L.I.S.T.E.N.ing Skills**—In Chapter 4 I introduced my acronym for L.I.S.T.E.N.ing. Here's a refresher:
   - **L** Look at the person you are talking to
   - **I** Interact when appropriate, but don't interrupt
   - **S** Say it back; repeat the information given
   - **T** Two-way communication
   - **E** Empathy Over Ego
   - **N** Nonverbal cues—body language matters

For me to have a constructive conversation with Jordan, I had to incorporate each of these aspects into our conversation. My nonverbal behavior was equally as important as the words I chose and the tone I used. My goal was to find a resolution that improved Jordan's hygiene. I made sure to listen to his reasoning first, which was essentially not doing laundry often enough, before I offered a solution. I took care not to introduce any other emotions or any other possible reasons for the odor that would diminish the success of this conversation. I listened and stuck to the point.

The most important fact to remember is that you have a choice as to how you want to respond during difficult conversations. Be intentional, be prepared, be compassionate, be authentic, and most of all, be present and listen.

SUCCESS TIP

It's important to check in with yourself and your actions. Self-ownership is key to maintaining self-control and credibility. Try this tip: Grab a Post-It Note or open the Notes app on your computer. Write a reminder message to yourself that says: "Empathy Over Ego." Keep this affirmation in a place where you can glance at it frequently. This is a great reminder and helpful tool when working through a variety of challenging interactions.

CHAPTER 9

POLISH YOUR PHONE SKILLS

Eric pensively walked through an impressive array of shiny new cars. The latest sedans, minivans, and SUVs appeared like a family of peacocks with their beautiful tails fanned out, trying to impress a mate, or in the case of this dealership, a new buyer. The familiar smell of new leather floated through the showroom floor.

My IT company had serviced this dealership for more than a decade. This time though, Eric was not here to support the network.

Greg, the owner, called Eric to talk about some service concerns. Assuming the discussion would be technical in nature, Eric prepared for this meeting by reviewing a variety of service-related requests and getting updates from our technicians.

He reached Greg's familiar office and peeked his head in. A sleek black desk sat in front of a large window. Perched on the windowsill was what appeared to be a family photo and a model of an antique Corvette.

Refocusing back to Greg's desk, Eric noticed a small stack of what appeared to be blank contracts next to a cylindrical pen holder that held logoed pens.

"Hey, Eric." Greg motioned for Eric to take one of the two gray mesh chairs in front of his desk.

"Hello Greg! How is the family?" Eric replied.

"Great, keeping me busy!"

"I hear you. My girls are eight and 10 but it feels like they're 18!"

They both chuckled.

Eric sat up in his chair, looked at Greg, and asked in a concerned voice, "So, tell me what's going on. Why did you want to talk?"

Greg's face turned serious. Eric thought he saw a bit of disappointment in his eyes. "It's time to part ways, Eric. We appreciate all that you and the team have done for us over the past 10 years, but we need a change."

"A change?" Eric repeated. "Will you please give me some feedback? I'm sorry we took a bit longer to get that new server project complete. We've made changes to our process so that won't happen again."

"That was disappointing, Eric, and I'm glad you're improving the process, but the biggest reason is your customer service. You don't make us feel special. Every time I call, your dispatcher acts like he doesn't know who I am."

Eric was speechless. He was ready to have a technical conversation, but the reality was our phone skills were abysmal. "I am so sorry, Greg, and thank you for bringing this to my attention. Is there anything I can do to change your mind? I truly value you and our relationship," Eric probed.

"Sorry, we've felt this way for a few months and have found someone to replace you. I am hoping you will cooperate during the transition."

"Of course we will, Greg. We'll do what we can. Again, I am sorry we let you down. That was never our intention."

"Best of luck, Eric," Greg said in a sincere tone.

"Thank you, Greg. It's been a pleasure servicing your dealership over the years." Eric stood up to shake Greg's hand.

Eric walked back to his car, this time not noticing the cars on the showroom floor. Back behind the wheel, he said out loud, "Really? You are firing us because we don't make you feel special on the phone? Seriously?"

Anger seeped through his veins and his blood began to boil. Part of his anger was at being fired, but the real brunt of his anger was at himself for brushing a known problem under the rug. This procrastination and apathy just cost our business over $15,000 a year.

No longer could this issue be pushed aside. It was time to make cultural changes, starting with our phones.

Why Care About Phone Skills?

A costly result of poorly answered phones: Your client or prospect calls your competitor.

How much patience do you have waiting on hold for 15 minutes for a service technician? How do you feel when you call an online retailer to order a new shirt and the employee on the other end speaks in an arrogant tone?

After nearly thirty years in business, I've narrowed down the four primary reasons our business phones ring:

1. A client is calling to place an order or with a service request.

2. A vendor is calling looking to establish or enhance a relationship.

3. A prospect is having an emergency and doesn't have a reliable service provider to reach out to or has no provider at all.

4. A prospect is dissatisfied with their current service provider or product and is in search of someone or something new.

In a small business, everyone is a salesperson, regardless of their title. The entire company must be prepared to answer the phone using the same script and upbeat tone of voice.

I've done the math and discovered it costs my small IT business around $500 just to get the phone to ring. $500! Consider how much money you could lose *or have lost* due to poorly answering/triaging a call or worse—not answering the call at all.

A *first impression* of a business is often set the moment a phone call is answered. Brand building starts here. How you, your receptionist, dispatcher, or anyone on your team answers the phone and ultimately makes that person calling *feel* determines next steps: a meeting, a new order, or hanging up and calling your competitor.

Do the math. What does it cost, meaning how much money are you spending on marketing, advertising, staffing, etc., to get a lead to call your business? Now, multiply that number by 12 potentially bungled calls (one per month).

For my IT business, that looks like $500 x 12 = $6,000

That is just the math for our cost-per-lead. I also want your mind to go one step further and think about the "lifetime" value of a new client. Think about the initial sales opportunity and multiply that number by the number of years a typical client stays with you and how much they spend with you over time.

My stomach turns, as I hope yours does too, when I think back to the car dealership that fired us, primarily due to our perceived disinterest in building relationships because of our poor phone skills. That client was paying us $15,000 per year. Not only did we miss out on that recurring revenue, but we also lost out on upsell opportunities, including helping them with the IT for the brand new dealership they had just built, and any referrals they might have sent our way.

Do you see now why phone skills matter? Can you imagine the revenue lost and reputational damage caused by not showing empathy and making your caller feel like a VIP? I hope so.

The Human Elements Needed for Great Phone Skills

Before I dialed the number, I took a deep breath. It was my turn to call Ramona and ask when the cushions for our new outdoor couch, side chair, and ottoman would be arriving.

Eric and I were excited to buy new outdoor furniture. We arrived at the reputable, family-owned outdoor furniture store that specialized in quality, high-end brands in March. We discovered the furniture was indeed high quality. Sadly, their customer service was anything but.

The day of our big purchase, Eric and I gasped at the amazing display on the showroom floor, including colorful outdoor umbrellas that looked like giant attendees at a fabulous outdoor party. There were dining tables made of glass, teak wood couches with matching coffee tables, and many wicker sets.

We made a significant purchase that day. We intended to buy only an outdoor dining table. However, we walked out with the table, eight matching chairs, a new teak couch, coffee table, two matching side chairs, and an ottoman. We even ordered matching custom-made striped cushions, for the dining seats and ottoman and solid-blue cushions for the couch and side chairs.

Ramona ably assisted us in selecting furniture and answering our many questions about durability and product care. She helped us sift through an endless rainbow of color swatches for seat cushions. She even provided us with a rough estimate of eight weeks for delivery. Eric and I provided a deposit and left. We were excited to plan a BBQ with friends to break in the new furniture.

Call #1—The first week of May Eric called to check on delivery. Ramona's son Mark picked up the phone and spoke in a fast-paced, inaudible tone.

Eric said, "Hello, may I speak to Ramona? I'd like to check the status of an order I placed two months ago."

After several seconds of silence on the other end, Mark finally said, "Ramona is busy helping another customer, can she call you back?"

Eric, trying to be understanding, said, "Can you check my status?"

"No, Ramona will do it." Mark answered, in an *It's not my job* tone of voice.

Feeling annoyed at the lack of support, Eric left his cell number and asked Ramona to call him back. "I'm an over $10,000 customer and Mark just treated me like I was just anyone calling," Eric told me. "He didn't even ask my name."

Call #2—One week later. Eric had not heard back from Ramona. He dialed the store again. This time, Ramona answered, in a somewhat friendlier tone than Mark. Eric again asked about our order status. This time, Ramona said, "I am going to have to call you back. I'm working with a client on the showroom floor."

Eric, feeling slighted, replied, "I'd just like an update on my order. You quoted me eight weeks. Do you have an ETA?"

Ramona sighed. "I'll have to let you know. I've got to get back to the other client. I'll call you later today." Click.

Eric was enraged!

Call #3—A few days later. This time Ramona did call, saying, "I have good and bad news. I have your furniture and can schedule delivery; however, I don't have your cushions. Those should be here by end of June. I'd like to process your next payment."

Eric provided his credit card number and scheduled the delivery of the furniture.

Call #4—End of June. I called Ramona and said, trying to be friendly, "We love the furniture, Ramona. Any word on the cushions?"

Without a hint of empathy or apology for the extreme delay, Ramona replied, "I hope they are here by the beginning of July."

Feeling panicked, I said, "We planned a party for mid-July and need the cushions for the party. Can you get any confirmation from the manufacturer?"

"I am doing the best I can," Ramona retorted. "We've been very busy."

"I'm happy you're busy, but we are great clients too," I said in a defensive yet calm tone. "I don't feel like you are taking our order seriously."

"We are. We are just busy and have so many orders." Ramona replied. End of that call.

Call #5—End of August. Eric called again, same non-urgent response: "I'll let you know." Eric even went into the store seeking answers, and I'm sure you can guess the response.

Call #6 (or whatever number at this point!)—It's now one year later. My turn to make the call. I am anticipating the same non-empathetic response. "Hi Ramona, I'm wondering what happened to our pillows. It's now six months later. Can you fulfill the order or not? Please just answer our question."

"Apparently, the manufacturer ran out of fabric and had a hard time sourcing it. But I found some and am having the rest of the order made up. I'll call you when they are in."

As of this writing, I have the cushions for the dining table chairs, ottoman, and couch. I am still waiting on cushions for our side chairs. I know Covid shifted lead times, but there is no excuse for the lack of responsiveness and desire to please a high-ticket customer.

Have you experienced service like this before? I hope not! Don't follow Ramona's lead when building brand credibility.

Instead, focus on these key areas. Think of phone skills like a calm W.A.V.E. Your intention is to keep the conversation flowing while ensuring your client feels calm and reassured for the entire talk.

W What's your name?

A Avoid apathy

V Vary your voice

E Emotional intelligence

W—What's Your Name? One of the keys to establishing an initial connection with a prospect is by simply saying their name. There is magic when we hear our name used in positive ways.

Whenever you can, learn your prospects' and clients' names, repeat them frequently, and make an effort to recognize their voices when they call. Teach your team to do the same.

A—Avoid Apathy. Instead, apply empathy. Each time Eric and I called the furniture store, we were treated like a distraction, not a respected client. There was no attempt to be apologetic for the horrendous timelines, nor did Ramona show any urgency when told of our upcoming party. Maybe she could have offered some "loaner cushions" or invited us to come back to the store to select a new fabric that was easier to source. Instead, we got a recurring excuse that they were too busy servicing other clients to figure out what was going on with our order. Possessing and displaying empathy is paramount to building trust. It is non-negotiable in any business environment.

V—Vary Your Voice. Please refer to the vocal foundations in Chapter 8, Dynamic Dialog. It's important to align your words and tone of voice to each unique conversation. Always answer the phone in a positive, upbeat tone. Then, after listening to the nature of the call, modulate your voice to demonstrate empathy, validation, and understanding. Be mindful of a monotone inflection—it can be misconstrued as disinterest. If the caller is having an emergency, show concern in your voice. If the caller is checking on the status of a delayed order, use an apologetic tone and demonstrate urgency in getting the matter resolved. Show enthusiasm for first-time callers and exciting news!

E—Exercise Emotional Intelligence (EQ). As a refresher, emotional intelligence is our ability to manage our emotions.

It's also our ability to recognize, understand, and positively influence other people's emotions through impactful and persuasive responses. Great phone conversations are the result of managing our emotions and speaking in a manner that supports the conversation, no matter if it is during difficult conversations, negotiations, sales conversations . . . even interviews.

Consistent Scripts

Morgan sits behind the reception desk of a bustling hair salon. Her friendly smile and welcoming voice make each client feel like a VIP when they walk through the glass door. She takes as much care on the phone as she does in person.

The salon's owner, Monika, knows "the phones" are the first impression of her salon and critical to ensure that a new client calling is placed with the correct stylist. She spent time training Morgan on the "lifetime value" of each client. She demonstrated: The average client spend on a visit is $125. They book appointments every six weeks. That's about nine visits per year, or $1,125. Most of our clients stay with us at least 10 years or more. That's a value of $11,250. Also remember, they'll buy products in the salon, and if they are happy, refer their friends and family to us.

Let's break down what I call the G.A.I.N. Method. This script is designed to provide consistency and demonstrate interest, as you gain the respect of the caller.

- **G—Greet caller with the time of the day**. "Good morning . . . afternoon . . . evening." This is a nice way to prime the call. It gives the caller an opportunity to hear your voice and establish a vocal connection.

SUCCESS EXERCISE

Calculate the average lifetime value of your clients. Use my example above. First, calculate the average value of your clients. Then, multiply that number by the average number of years they stay with your business. What is the "total lifetime value" of your client? Finally, ask yourself, can you afford NOT to put an emphasis on how you answer your phones and triage each call?

- **A—Appreciate the caller.** Imagine each call coming into your business as an opportunity to make a sale. With that opportunity, why wouldn't you take special interest in handling each call? I know some calls to your business are unwelcome. But how you handle each call can either build or sever a critical relationship. Continue your greeting with "thank you for calling (your company name)."
- **I—Identify yourself.** Establish that initial connection by introducing yourself and sharing your name. As I've mentioned, our name is one of the first words we learn. It's special to us. When someone learns and says our name, it's a wonderful and cordial way to set the tone for a personal relationship.
- **N—Next step.** The final component of the initial greeting is to ask, "How can I help you?" The mindset behind this question is "How can I make your day better today?" "How

can I service you to help you or your business?" "How can I give you peace of mind?")

THE INITIAL GREETING SCRIPT

Monika explained this process to Morgan. "This is the script we use here. Depending on the time of day, say, *"Good morning, thank you for calling Coiffed Salon. Morgan speaking. How may I help you?"*

Monika asked Morgan to recite the script a couple of times to get used to saying it and listen for upbeat energy in her voice.

QUALIFY BEFORE YOU DISQUALIFY THAT LEAD

"Great job, Morgan!" Monika exclaimed. "I love how you added your friendly personality into your voice. Now let's talk about how to qualify and triage each client, whether new or existing. Not every stylist is going to be a good fit for each client. By asking a series of questions, you'll have a better sense of who to schedule with whom. Here are the questions I want you to ask to qualify each caller":

1. If a new client calls, ask:

    a. First say, "I am so glad you called! May I have your first and last name and address?"
    b. Next, "In case we get disconnected, may I have your phone number and email address?"
    c. "How did you hear about us?" (An important marketing question so you can thank the person who gave you the referral or spend more advertising dollars there.)

d. (Say caller's name, then ask): "So I can learn more about you:

  i. "Tell me about your hair. Is it thick, thin, curly, straight, long, or short?"
  ii. "Are you looking for a new color or looking to color correct your hair?"
  iii. "Tell me about your experience at other salons."

e. "When were you looking to come into the salon?"

2. Now say, "Thank you (say caller's name) for all that information. Let me look at the schedule now."

3. For an existing client say, "Hi, (caller's name!). It's great to hear from you. How can I help you?"

Putting the Caller on Hold

Monika continued her phone skills training with: "If you have to put a client on hold to talk to a stylist or check schedules, please say, 'I need to talk to the stylist, would it be OK if I put you on hold, or would you prefer I call you back?' We want to show courtesy to our clients—that we care about their time, and we don't want them to have to wait on the line, any longer than they have to."

Avoid statements like "Please hold" and then abruptly put the caller on hold. Courtesy counts here.

The Voice Message

Monika finished with one last important script. "As part of our follow-up process, we have a standard voice message for when calling to confirm a client's appointment. If they don't answer their phone, please say, '*Hi (client's name), this is Morgan from Coiffed Salon. I am calling to confirm your (time of appointment) on (day of week and date) with (stylist name). If you can't make this appointment, please call our salon at (555-555-5555) and let's get you rescheduled! I look forward to seeing you soon!*"

No Blind Transfers!

"Oh, I almost forgot to review one more process," Monika said. Sometimes, calls will come in for me or asking to speak to one of the stylists. If I am with a client, please take a message. If I am not and able to take the call, please do not do a "blind transfer to me."

Monika looked at Morgan's confused expression and knew she needed to explain. "A blind transfer is when a call is taken and then transferred to me without me knowing who the caller on the other end is or why they are calling. I'd like to be discerning with calls coming in. A new client or a client with an issue will take precedent over a vendor calling. So please be sure to ask:

- Who is calling, first and last name and company name, if applicable.
- The nature of their call.
- The best phone number to call them back at, in case we get disconnected.

"I always make sure that when I then pick up the call, I say the caller's name and repeat the nature of the issue. An example is: 'Hi, June! Morgan tells me you had an issue with your stylist.

SUCCESS EXERCISE

As Monika demonstrated, having standardized scripts in your business will help eliminate inconsistencies in how each employee answers the phone, and it creates the necessary standardization and uniformity your clients crave. Now it's your turn. Open a new document on your computer. Using the scripts I provided above, modify each one to be used in your organization.

- Standard Greeting Script
- Qualifying Questions to Triage the Caller and New Prospect
- Putting the Caller on Hold
- Never Blind Transfer—What questions should you ask before you transfer a call? And how do you want the call answered when it is transferred to an employee?
- The Voice Message—What standard message do you want your employee to leave if they are calling to follow up on an appointment?

What other standard phone scripts can you document? The more you have, the easier it is to train future employees and course-correct existing employees when they stray from your established process.

Can you tell me more about your experience?' I want the client to feel like a VIP and using their name goes a long way."

Morgan role-played each of the scripts with Monika. Monika made sure to make Morgan aware of the vocal ranges she needed to use to sound excited and to show empathy.

Morgan eventually memorized the scripts and process, but is grateful to have everything on one sheet to continuously refer to.

SUCCESS EXERCISE

Say This Instead

A great tool to use with your team to practice phone skills and discuss various scenarios that occur regularly in your business is the "Say This Instead" exercise. The table below shows a series of common reasons why someone calls your business. Use these scenarios as the foundation for your conversation starters. Feel free to modify each to better suit your business.

Have one person read the "Situation." Next, say the "Don't Say This . . ." response, putting emphasis on the words and vocal ranges that would NOT be appropriate to build strong relationships.

Finally, say the "Instead, Say This . . ." response in a tone of voice that sounds confident and interested in helping the caller.

Discuss the differences between the "Don't Say This . . ." statement and the "Instead, Say This . . ." statement. Emphasize and reinforce the positive statements and tones of voice. Refer to this exercise quarterly to remind your team to remember you take the handling of phone calls seriously.

Situation	Don't Say This . . .	Instead, Say This . . .
A new call comes into your business; an employee answers the call . . .	"(Company name), can I help you?"	"Good morning, thank you for calling (your company), (name speaking), how can I help you?"
A frustrated client is calling because they have not heard back regarding the status of their order placed over a week ago.	"We've been busy . . ." "I haven't heard back from my supplier . . ." "I know you are frustrated but . . ."	Two answers: "I am sorry for the delay. Let me see what is going on so I can get you a status update. Can I call you back in a few minutes?" (Even if you don't have an answer, call them back and let them know.)
A client calls about the status of a service request. You must put the client on hold, to talk to the technician to check status.	"Hold on a second." "Give me a minute." "Please hold."	"Client name, I'd like to research that request. May I put you on hold for a minute, or would you prefer that I call you back?"
You did not hear the last few words of a client's request.	"What did you say?" "You want me to do what?"	"I'm sorry, client name, I missed hearing that last request. Would you please repeat it?"
A client is asking you to implement a new technology you've never worked on before.	"It's not something we do." "I don't know if we can do it." "I'm not sure . . ."	"We haven't worked on this yet, but I want to help you. Let me do some research and I'll get back to you with a plan and suggestions."

5 Email Errors and How to Correct Them

While most of this chapter focuses on impeccable phone skills, I'd be remiss if I didn't dedicate a special section to **Email Etiquette**. Have you ever received an email and thought, "Is this person angry with me?" or "So many typos . . . maybe their work is sloppy too?"

Years ago, I was buying advertising space on a popular local radio show. The sales representative I was working with was friendly in person, but when it came to email, she was anything but. I perceived her tone as annoyed. She used words and phrases such as "Obviously," and "OK, let me reiterate . . ." How does each of those email openers make you feel? What impression have they left on you?

Picking up the phone and making a call is the most important tool for relationship building. Email, however, is also part of our everyday workday. The problem with email is that it's one-dimensional. You are just reading words on a page. It's easy to misinterpret the intent of a message, but hearing and understanding your tone of voice is much harder to get wrong.

Let's look at five common email errors I see consistently. If you are the culprit for any of these, please take note. You could be putting your hard-earned brand in jeopardy. Read and reflect on the following suggestions on how to correct them.

Error #1—Using Passive Words That Diminish Leadership Credibility

Here are a few words that will easily shift a client or a prospect's perspective of you.

No Confidence Word	Shows Confidence
But	Use *And* instead. "I like your report, *AND* I think by adding this graph, it'll provide even more data."
Hopefully	"Let me do some research."
Basically	Remove this word altogether.
Try	As Yoda said, "There is no try, only do!" Don't sound unsure. Let the prospect know you'll do some research and get back to them.
Can't / No / I Don't Know	**Caution:** Before you say any of these, research first. Set the expectation that you will "look into the best solution" and get back to them with a response. A quick *no* or *we can't do that*, will lower the confidence level.

Error #2—Grammar Goof-ups

Several common words are often misspelled or used incorrectly in a sentence. Discuss with your team the differences between each word below and the correct time to use each. If you don't know, please research the definition of each. You'll find the correct answer in parenthesis at the end of each statement.

- I didn't do **nothing** or **anything** with your project yet. (anything)
- **Its** or **It's** a beautiful day. (It's)
- **Your** or **You're** welcome. (You're)
- I **seen** or **saw** her bring in the computer yesterday. (saw)

- I don't know **were** or **where** to add the folder. (where)
- My **company's** or **companies'** goals are set. (company's)
- I like the new office **to** or **too** or **two**? (too)
- The new data does not **affect** or **effect** the outcome of the report. (affect)
- What would you add to this list?

Error #3—Email Is Too Long, Too Short, or Contains Emotional Language

We are busy, distracted people. Sometimes, email messages are too long winded, vague, or emotional, i.e., they appear to convey anger or impatience. Quick answers like "I need that report tomorrow" can lead to many questions. Which report? What time tomorrow? What data do you need in that report? The questions could be endless and frustrating.

Maintain credibility by sending concise, friendly responses. Be specific. Say, "May I please have that payroll report by end of day tomorrow?" It's friendlier, gives more detail, and includes the time of day you'd like to receive the report. Also, the follow-up questions can be more direct and in line with what you are looking for.

Error #4—Using All CAPS Too Much (or Too Little) Punctuation

"I'D LIKE THAT REPORT TOMORROW!!!!!" What is your first impression of this subject line? It's likely to be anger or frustration. Perhaps the sender was thinking, *"I don't see anything wrong here. I am so busy and just needed to send a quick message."*

Perception is reality. Your quick response can easily be misconstrued, and that misperception can potentially be carried over to the work you do.

Error #5—Missing Friendly Salutations and Signatures

It's worth taking a few extra seconds to start your emails with *Hello (name), Hi (name), Good morning (name), or Dear (name).* It warms up and sets the tone of your email. It's also best to end your messages on a friendly note. *Warm regards; Thank you so much; Sincerely;* or whatever friendly closing you prefer demonstrates an attempt to be welcoming, maintains relationship consistency, and shows that you care about the details.

SUCCESS EXERCISE

Review email errors with your team. Use actual emails from your office. Referencing the suggestions above, ask the team, "What do you think of the tone of this email?" "What do you notice about the grammar?" "How can it be reworded or edited to sound friendlier?"

CHAPTER 10

DOES YOUR DIGITAL PRESENCE ALIGN WITH YOUR IN-PERSON PRESENCE?

THE STATISTICS

In all honesty, I have mixed feelings about having an online presence. I'm referring to your website and social media profiles. My colleague Emily summed up much of my apprehension with "being online" when she said, "For most people, our online presence is NOT who we are, it's who we want people to think we are."

How often do you find yourself scrolling through someone's personal or business social feed, sighing while feeling defeated, and softly muttering, "Wow, this person's life and career are so perfect, do they ever have a bad day?" Imposter syndrome slams the door on the last bit of confidence you cling to.

Another extreme is having zero online presence. How will your clients and prospects find you and learn about your new (and old) products and services? If they research you, what will they find?

Or maybe you have an online presence, for example, on LinkedIn, but your page is missing a headshot, and your last post was about a golf tournament you attended five years ago. How will your clients and prospects get to know who you are today?

The pressure, the falsehood, the lack of *integrity*; the social media brand building struggle is real.

Does keeping up your digital presence send you on an emotional roller coaster? Does your stomach ache as you think about the massive power social media has over making or breaking your brand?

OK. Enough talk about the downside. Take a deep breath and let's move on.

There is a huge upside to putting effort into your online presence. Instead of closing your door, you are opening it wide and inviting your target audience to come on in and learn more.

According to **Hootsuite's Digital 2022 Global Overview report**, there are 4.95 billion internet users. Of that astounding number, 4.62 billion of them are active on social media. That is a massive door of opportunity, no matter your business size.

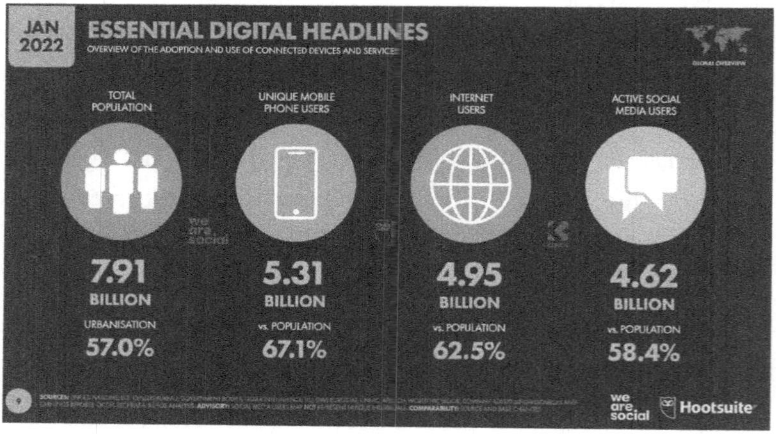

You might be thinking, "Geez, Lisa, I don't want to reach billions of people."

I get you! Here is where my marketing degree comes in. Here's how to think more strategically and narrow your focus. First, take a deep breath and know you don't have to be everywhere—just where your clients and prospects are spending time.

Let's start by doing a short but critical exercise to identify your target audience. Determining who your client is will help you determine where your online focus should be.

First, create a table like the example below. You may not have a specific industry focus, although this is a key factor in building your credibility, but I know you will have enough insight to fill in the table below.

Industry	Psychographic: What keeps them up at night? Their beliefs and attitudes?	Demographic: What is their age, gender, and occupation?	Geographic: Where do they live and work?
Example: Legal	Billing clients and time entry Flexibility in securely accessing client files online Etc.	My target age range is: 45-65 Title/Role: Managing Partner	New England
Your answer here:	Your answer here:	Your answer here:	Your answer here:

Next, check out Hootsuite's **Digital 2022: The Global State of Digital 2022 Top Takeaways** breakdown by age group in their **"Top Channels for Online Brand Research"** chart below. Now, find your target audience. Do they prefer to do their research via search engines such as Google Chrome, Bing, and Safari? Or are they more apt to gain brand awareness from social sites such as Facebook, Instagram, TikTok, or LinkedIn?

Rule of thumb when building a Personal Brand: *You need to be where your audience is. So open that door!*

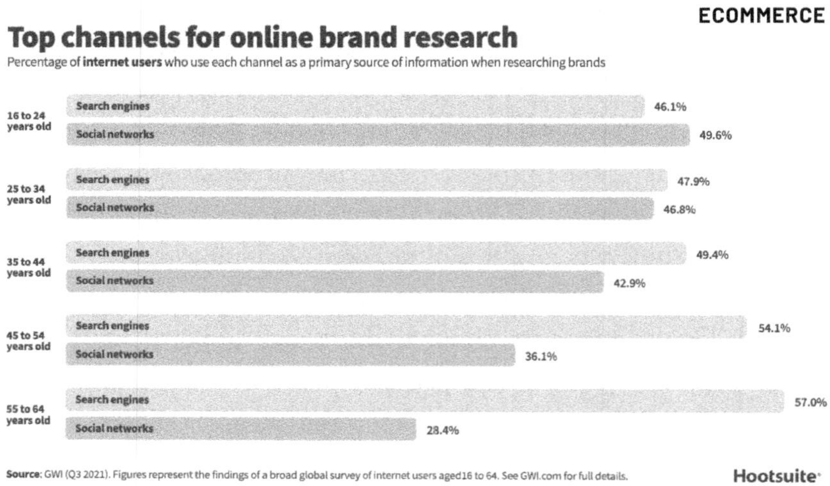

B.R.A.N.D. Unity to Avoid B.R.A.N.D. Ambiguity

In Chapter 3, I mentioned my 3 C's of Image—Consistency, Congruency, and Credibility. These comprise the foundation of your online presence. Is your online presence consistent with your office appearance, your and your team's in-person appearance, invoices, products produced, messaging, etc.?

You *are* being searched. It's part of the discovery process. Your clients and prospects are looking to see your posts, comments, and what others are saying about you. So, does your online activity build your brand or leave your followers or would-be followers confused?

From Confusion to Clarity

I was hired by Jake, a talented yet frustrated owner of a small IT company, to help him gain more confidence in sharing his unique story, both in-person and online. He was tired of being perceived as just the "IT Guy" and not a true business partner.

In a pleading tone he asked me, "How do I differentiate myself from my competitors? I not only have technical understanding, I also have Chief Financial Officer experience working for other businesses that many of my peers don't have. I bring a business perspective to my solutions, not just a technical one. I stumble articulating this during the sales process—when I can get the phone to ring, that is."

He sighed and added, "If I am not clear how to articulate this in person, I certainly can't write about it online. My LinkedIn profile hasn't been updated in years, nor has my website."

We agreed that I would help him create a compelling story to enable him to communicate his value as not just an "IT Guy" but a true "Trusted Advisor" who excels at solving business problems.

We began by crafting an elevator pitch that concisely said what Jake did and what made him unique.

Next, we focused on his website and rewrote his "Home Page" message, his "About Jake" page, and the "Industries I Serve" pages to ensure it was clear that he understood his clients' pain points and how his technical and C-Level experience would help his clients leverage technology to grow their business.

SUCCESS EXERCISE

Spend time crafting your unique story. What experiences or people in your life made you an authority or expert in your industry? Next, assess your current website. Does it convey your values and expertise? Finally, perform a Google search on yourself. What will the researcher learn about you? Does it align with your unique story?

LinkedIn for Leaders—Focus on these 5 Areas of Your Profile

Once Jake's website was updated, we shifted to his LinkedIn profile. Jake knew LinkedIn is where his clients and prospects are found. Yet he had never really taken the time to put any effort into building a profile that clearly reflected who he was and how he wanted to be perceived by his connections and followers.

Stop! Is this you, too? Do you have a LinkedIn profile? If you do, when was the last time you updated the information?

LinkedIn has become known as the social media channel for professionals. As a professional in any industry, it is critical to have a presence here. Are you thinking, *my clients are also on Instagram and/or Facebook*. That's great, and you should put effort there too.

Let's make a deal. How about you focus on these five areas of your LinkedIn profile? That way, you have some social media brand consistency.

1. **Professional Headshot**—Say a confident "hello" to your visitor with a great headshot. Take the time to have professional shots done. If budget is an issue, set your mobile phone's camera to "portrait mode" to snap a picture. Make sure you are professionally dressed and groomed from the waist up, with neat hair; teeth brushed and flossed; moisturizer for men and women; ladies, a bit of make-up to brighten your face. You can't fit that much in that little circle, but boy does it set the tone of the perception of your entire page!

   I've seen professional people use fuzzy images, pictures of half of their face, shots taken from several feet away, or those that have happy images arm in arm with friends or loved ones, making it hard to tell who the actual profile is for. Makes you wonder, are they serious professionals?

But the biggest culprit is not taking the time to add any picture at all. At least the other offenders show some effort was made.

2. **Keyword-Friendly Headline**—Now that you have a fabulous and professional-looking headshot uploaded to your profile, it's time to write your Profile Headline right below it. After that first glance of your face, the eyes drop to your description. For my client Jake, all his description said was "CEO of XYZ Company." Boring! I explained to Jake that this is an opportunity to show some personality and expertise to his (and your) followers and include key search terms that his (and your) prospects use to search you via LinkedIn. Another bonus—it impacts Google search results. What two to three industry keywords are your prospects using to find you online? Are there products or services you sell that will make your profile stand out from others'? What do you stand for? Who is your target audience? What is your personality? Ask all these questions when writing your description.

   With Jake, I used my husband Eric's header as a visual example: *President | IT Expert for Law Firms, Property Management & Small Businesses | Office 365 Guru | Video Security Expert | Cybersecurity*

   I shared mine too: *Image Consultant | Expert Corporate & Personal Brand Coach | Managed Services Provider Business Owner | Motivational Speaker & Marketing Maven | Author*

One more tip: Don't make it too long. While you have space for 220 characters, this is not the time to write a paragraph. Save the broader details for your Profile's "About" summary.

3. **Profile "About" Section**—This is your chance to tell your story. Introduce yourself to your viewers and what is important to you. Use a statement like this as you prepare your About section structure: "I am the coolest cat around (powerful opener), this is why we should connect or work together (sum up your experience from past to present), and here is a way to contact me (call-to-action)."

   Keep in mind, when writing this section, it should be first person, as if you are "speaking directly to" your viewers. Include some keyword search terms that your audience may use to find you—software they use, different tools, languages, etc. This is not a resume but an extension of your Personal Brand, so be careful not to be too robotic in your writing. If you need some help here, enlist the editing skills of a friend or colleague.
   - Ask them, how would you jazz this up?
   - What did you learn about me?
   - Can you tell what is important to me?

4. **Work Experience**—This section is most like a resume. Viewers want to know your work history, so add your experience. Do yourself a favor and add a few words about what you **accomplished** at each position. Remember,

you are building your brand without being in front of a person. Sometimes your online presence is all a prospective lead has to make a decision as to whether they call you or a competitor. Showcase the breadth of work you've done.

Image Tip: A great way to add pizzazz to your profile is to include a variety of links highlighting media interviews, podcasts you participated in, videos you created, and more. This will bring your work history and profile to life.

5. **Relevant Posts**—You've come this far, let's keep moving! You've built out your profile, whew. Now it's time to focus on posting. Your posts are meant to teach your business expertise and build your credibility as an expert in your field. Let's talk about what I call the "Social S.I.D.E." of Marketing.

Build Credibility—The Social S.I.D.E. of Things

Jake's earnest face looked at me through our virtual Microsoft Teams meeting. He shared, "I'm glad my website and LinkedIn profiles are updated. But I struggle with content. What do I post? I don't have anything to say."

"Jake," I replied in an empathetic tone, my eyes shifting to the camera lens to appear that I was looking directly at him, "you have so much to share. Use this acronym to help you get started. The 'S, I, and D' are ideas for content to post. The 'E' stands for ways for you to engage with others.

By the way—the Social S.I.D.E. should be applied to all your social media channels.

Share	– Company news – Clients' good news – Relevant news in the media that impacts your clients – Inspiring quotes
Invite	– Followers to a webinar you are hosting or attending – A Lunch and Learn – A client event – A volunteer community event
Direct	– To view a particular page of your website – To subscribe or follow you on other social channels. – To view a page on a colleague's website – To a registration page
Engage (comment on others' posts!)	– Create a post that asks a question and requests comments from readers. – Comment on your colleagues' posts that show your expertise, excitement, or empathy. – Join an online group and ask questions and comment on others' posts. – Send connection requests to build out your following, with personalized notes.

Don't Post That on Social Media

Jake's visible apprehension eased with each idea we added to his new content list. He then asked, "OK, Lisa, this is great. I am sure you have a list of content that I shouldn't post, right?"

"I sure do!" I said in a "how'd you guess" tone. "Not all content is good content, Jake. This is where intention versus interpretation can make a loyal follower unfollow you or worse, post something negative about you. Your reputation matters. It takes years to build a strong brand, and mere minutes to crush it!"

You want content (across all your social media channels) to showcase your expertise and your knowledge of your industries served. And please, steer clear of these credibility crushers:

- **Content About Religion**—This is a private subject that should be discussed in your home or house of worship. Not the workplace. An occasional "Happy Holidays" is fine, but anything more and you might offend that hot lead you've been trying to convert or a client who has different views than you.
- **Content About Politics**—See above for why!
- **Derogatory Language**—There is never a need to use derogatory language in the workplace or your online profiles. Period.
- **Negative Content**—There is a time and a place to provide "Reviews" of products and services you've received. Your business social channels are not that place. If you see someone else post something negative about you, it's your job to maintain your credibility by being diplomatic and polite.
- **Buy=Buy=Buy Content**—Some people make the mistake of only creating posts asking the viewer to "Buy Now." How will you develop a relationship and trust with the buyer? There is a place for selling on social, but this platform is primarily meant to build trust and convince your viewers to set up a meeting with you. Then you can work to convert those prospects into paying clients. Be mindful

not to skip the several critical steps I mentioned in the Social S.I.D.E. information. These are vital foundations in the cultivation process. Remember, people buy based on trust and emotion.

Time to Get Started!

Social media is so influential and widely used globally that you must embrace it! But you want to make sure you embrace it intentionally and focus on where your clients are.

Begin your social media journey, as in all your brand building efforts, by focusing on your Value Judgments exercise from Chapter 3. Align both your in-person and online presence.

Before you create a post, ask yourself two questions:

1. How do you want to be perceived by others?

2. Does this post/comment build my brand, confuse my brand, or is it so controversial that it will turn people away and make them unfollow me?

Great work! I'm proud of you. It's Time to Unleash Your B.R.A.N.D.!

SUCCESS EXERCISE

Keep the momentum going! Block off one to two hours on your calendar. Use the list above to update your LinkedIn profile. Do this same exercise for your other social media channels. Then, block off another one to two hours to create content, using the suggestions above. Finally, schedule the posts you created.

Conclusion

Congratulations! Picture me giving you a "high-five" right now! Better yet, give yourself a high-five. By reading this book, you set out on a journey very few will embark on.

You may have finished this book, but your adventure in unleashing your brand has just begun. Your path to Brand Building Rockstar status is now at a crossroads. It's time to make a pivotal career decision.

In the Introduction, I started with a mantra: *"Tech skills alone won't build my business."* Pause for a moment and say that statement out loud, with conviction. Please say it one more time.

Now you have a choice: Either put this book on the shelf with your other fabulous business books and say, "Well, that was a great read." Or you can do as poet Robert Frost famously wrote in his poem "The Road Not Taken":

> *Two roads diverged in a wood, and I—*
> *I took the one less traveled by,*
> *And that has made all the difference.*

Reaffirm your purpose and personal Core Value words. Then focus on turning my B.R.A.N.D. Method into your *new* mantras:

Behavior—I will consider my actions and emotional reactions when building trusting relationships.
Respect—I will make time to respect my well-being first, then focus on ways to respect my corporate brand and the brand of my clients.
Appearance—I will do a daily self-assessment to ensure my appearance aligns with my brand and conveys a message of confidence and credibility.
Networking—My team and I are intentionally seeking places to meet new prospects along with ensuring our actions consistently build rapport and credibility to turn my clients into raving fans.
Dynamic **D**ialogue—I will listen to the words I say and how I say them. I will be honest with myself. I will strive to have empathetic conversations that create brand loyalty.

You've taken the first step and read this book. You are on this earth to make a profound impact! Take your next step with pride. Hop out of the well of your comfort zone and unleash *your* B.R.A.N.D.—the brand your clients NEED right now.

Resources Roundup

Doug Lipp | Customer Service & Disney Institute Keynote Speaker. (2022, August 25). Doug Lipp. https://douglipp.com/

Address to Joint Session of Congress May 25, 1961 | JFK Library. (n.d.). https://www.jfklibrary.org/learn/about-jfk/historic-speeches/address-to-joint-session-of-congress-may-25-1961

Tony Robbins Quotes, Read These Empowering Quotes from Tony Robbins. (2022, November 1). tonyrobbins.com. https://www.tonyrobbins.com/tony-robbins-quotes/

George T. Doran, "There's a S.M.A.R.T. way to write management's goals and objectives," AMA Forum, November 1981, pg. 35

https://community.mis.temple.edu/mis0855002fall2015/files/2015/10/S.M.A.R.T-Way-Management-Review.pdf

Goleman, Daniel. (1995). *Emotional Intelligence: Why It Can Matter More Than IQ.* New York: Penguin Random House LLC.

Dr. Nido Qubein—*High Point University.* (2022, May 8). High Point University. https://www.highpoint.edu/faculty-staff/administration/nido-qubein/

Marcus Lemonis. (2023, August 15). *Marcus Lemonis Official Website & Learning Center.* https://marcuslemonis.com/

Holmes, Chet., Holmes, Amanda. (2007, 2022). *The Ultimate Sales Machine: Turbocharge Your Business With Relentless Focus On 12 Key Strategies,* Portfolio/Penguin

TEDx Talks. (2010, October 7). *TEDxToronto—Drew Dudley "Leading with Lollipops"* [Video]. YouTube. https://www.youtube.com/watch?v=hVCBrkrFrBE

image noun—Definition, pictures, pronunciation, and usage notes | Oxford Advanced American Dictionary at OxfordLearnersDictionaries.com. (n.d.). https://www.oxfordlearnersdictionaries.com/us/definition/american_english/image

Adam, H., & Galinsky, A. D. (2012). Enclothed cognition. *Journal of Experimental Social Psychology, 48*(4), 918–925. https://doi.org/10.1016/j.jesp.2012.02.008

Staff, E. M. E. (2018, April 26). Infographic: Five Scientific Reasons People Are Wired to Respond to Visual Marketing. *Entrepreneur.* https://www.entrepreneur.com/en-ae/marketing/infographic-five-scientific-reasons-people-are-wired-to/312551

MediaTrainingCompany. (2021, November 23). *Albert Mehrabian—Rare Interview—55-38-7 Rule vs. Myth* [Video]. YouTube. https://www.youtube.com/watch?v=bPi7GmQIjB8

TEDx Talks. (2018, May 22). *Vocal Branding: How your voice shapes your communication Image | Wendy LeBorgne | TEDxUCiNcinnati* [Video]. YouTube. https://www.youtube.com/watch?v=p_ylzGfHKOs

Kerwin Rae Podcast Clips. (2021, December 10). *The 5 Vocal Foundations of Great Communication | Vinh Giang on*

UNSTOPPABLE [Video]. YouTube. https://www.youtube.com/watch?v=CuaY4qe4V34

——. "Home—Roger Love." Roger Love, January 26, 2024. https://rogerlove.com/.

Michael W. Kraus, "Voice-Only Communication Enhances Empathic Accuracy," Yale University, School of Management (n.d.)

https://static1.squarespace.com/static/5432c0d8e4b0fc3eccdb0500/t/58a3af349f74565ea7d27f32/1487122231232/voice-only-communication-enhances-empathic-accuracy.pdf

Does your voice reveal more emotion than your face? Greater Good Magazine, Emma Seppala (June 19, 2017). https://greatergood.berkeley.edu/article/item/does_your_voice_reveal_more_emotion_than_your_face

Hootsuite Inc. (n.d.). *Digital Trends—Digital Marketing Trends 2022.* Digital Trends—Digital Marketing Trends 2022. https://www.hootsuite.com/resources/digital-trends

Digital-2022-Top-Takeaways.pdf. (n.d.). https://hootsuite.widen.net/s/xf2mbffsbq/digital-2022-top-takeaways

Digital2022GlobalOverview_Report_en.pdf. (n.d.). https://hootsuite.widen.net/s/kd6qgn9rwx/digital2022globaloverview_report_en

Appleton, B. (2021, February 4). 10 Social Media Fails to Avoid in 2021. *HubSpot.* Retrieved December 15, 2023, from https://blog.hubspot.com/marketing/avoid-social-media-fails

RobotIn. (2022, January 11). *How to create a good headline on LinkedIn. Examples of headers :).* https://www.linkedin.com/pulse/how-create-good-headline-linkedin-examples-headers-robotin/?trk=organization-update-content_share-article

About the Author

Lisa Shorr is the leading expert in unleashing your brand to multiply your sales. She is a Certified Image Consultant and Personal Branding Specialist who specializes in elevating the client experience for professional service companies with an immediate impact on their bottom line.

As the visionary owner of **Shorr Success** and co-owner of **Secure Future Tech Solutions**, Lisa embodies innovation and excellence. Her remarkable achievements include serving as Sales Manager at Houghton Mifflin and authoring the acclaimed book, "*Your B.R.A.N.D. Unleashed*."

Lisa's expertise extends beyond words. Certified in Advanced Image Consulting and Corporate Consultancy, she has developed the transformative "Shorr-to-Shine System." This powerful methodology empowers companies to exponentially increase their profits by unlocking effective systems for client communication.

A sought-after speaker, Lisa graces professional stages, podcasts, and webinars worldwide.

Her articles have appeared in prestigious publications such as *PC World*, *ChannelPro Magazine*, *MSP Success*, and *Providence Business News*, to name a few.

Lisa's focus on the "*human side of building a business*" sets her apart, and her proven **B.R.A.N.D. Method** creates brand integrity and loyalty that resonates with clients and audiences alike.

She lives in Rhode Island with her husband, Eric, and two daughters.

Your B.R.A.N.D. Unleashed
Power Pack!
$2,987
Value
FREE
Phone Scripts
Email Cheat
Sheet
$250 Off!
GIFT CARD
Work with me
and save!
Sales Starters
Claim Yours NOW! Visit:
www.yourbrandunleashedbonus.com